T0340300

The Pattern of Aid Giving

Practically all donor countries that give aid claim to do so partly on the basis of the recipient country's quality of governance, but do these claims have a real impact on the allocation of aid? Are democratic, human rights-respecting countries with low levels of corruption and military expenditures more likely to receive aid than other countries? Do they also receive more aid than other countries?

Using econometric analysis, the author examines the factors that determine the patterns of aid giving in the 1990s. Eric Neumayer analyses such examples as:

- aggregate aid flows
- aid from multilateral organisations such as the EC and the UN
- aid from bilateral donors such as Germany, Japan and the US as well as Arab donors.

This concise, well-argued and well-researched book will be a great read for students, academics and policy-makers involved in Development Studies, Economics and International Relations.

Eric Neumayer is Lecturer in Environment and Development at the London School of Economics, UK.

Routledge studies in development economics

The Pattern of Aid Giving

The impact of good governance
on development assistance

Eric Neumayer

Routledge
Taylor & Francis Group

LONDON AND NEW YORK

First published 2003
by Routledge
2 Park Square, Milton Park, Abingdon, Oxon, OX14 4RN

Simultaneously published in the USA and Canada
by Routledge
605 Third Avenue, New York, NY 10017

Routledge is an imprint of the Taylor & Francis Group, an informa business

Typeset in Times New Roman by
Newgen Imaging Systems (P) Ltd, Chennai, India

British Library Cataloguing in Publication Data
A catalogue record for this book is available from the British Library

Library of Congress Cataloging in Publication Data
Neumayer, Eric, 1970–
    The pattern of aid giving : the impact of good governance on
development assistance / Eric Neumayer.
        p. cm. – (Routledge studies in development economics,
ISSN 1359-7884 ; 34)
    Includes bibliographical references and index.
    1. Economic assistance – Political aspects. 2. Economic assistance –
Econometric models. 3. Conditionality (International relations)
4. Democracy – Developing countries. 5. Human rights – Developing
countries. I. Title. II. Series.

HC60 .N472 2003
338.91–dc21   2002036918

ISBN13: 978–0–415–29811–7 (hbk)
ISBN13: 978–0–415–40695–6 (pbk)

Contents

Tables

Preface

Has good governance been rewarded in the allocation of aid in the 1990s? This question is at the heart of this book. Laymen and laywomen often think that to answer such a question is rather straightforward and that all one needs to do is to see how much aid is given to countries that fare high on some measure of governance compared to those that perform badly. Unfortunately, things are not quite so simple. On the most basic level, for example, one needs to control for the impact of other variables. Failure to account for these other variables could lead to distorted conclusions. These and other complications necessitate the use of sometimes rather complex statistical estimation techniques. An unfortunate consequence is that an analysis, which employs such techniques, becomes less accessible to readers than one would hope for.

Nevertheless, I hope to have written a book that is understandable to most students, policy makers and activists in the wider aid and development community even if they do not have major statistical training. I have tried to keep technical jargon to a minimum and to explain technical concepts wherever possible. Still, those without any knowledge of statistics might want to skip the first part of Chapter 4. For these readers it is sufficient to understand that we need to distinguish between two stages of the aid allocation by all those donors, which do not give some positive, if often small, amount of aid to all recipient countries. For these donors there is an aid eligibility stage, where the main objective is to assess whether good performance in terms of governance raises the likelihood of being eligible for aid. And then there is also a level stage, where the main objective is to analyse whether countries that score high on aspects of good governance receive more aid than other eligible countries. For the other donors, which give some aid to all or almost all countries, there is no need to address the aid eligibility stage and we can concentrate on the level stage right away.

This book would not have been possible without the help and the constructive comments of many people. I will not list names here even more because many of them have been anonymous reviewers of the book proposal itself as well as of some prior work published in academic journals.

Dr Eric Neumayer
London School of Economics and Political Science
London, January 2003

Abbreviations

2SLS	Two-stage least squares
ACP	Africa, Caribbean and Pacific
ARPP	Portfolio Performance Rating
COV	Covariance
CPIA	Country Policy and Institutional Assessment
DAC	Development Assistance Committee
DI	Donor interest
EC	European Community
EDA	Effective development assistance
EU	European Union
FDI	Foreign direct investment
GDP	Gross domestic product
GG	Good governance
GLS	Generalised least squares
GNI	Gross national income
GNP	Gross national product
HDI	Human development index
ICRG	International country risk guide
IDA	International Development Association
IMF	International Monetary Fund
IMR	Infant mortality rate
IV	Instrumental variables
LE1	Life expectancy at age one
OA	Official assistance
ODA	Official development assistance
OECD	Organisation for Economic Co-operation and Development
OLS	Ordinary least squares
OPEC	Organisation of Petroleum Exporting Countries
PPP	Purchasing power parity
PQLI	Physical quality of life index

PTS	Political terror scales
RN	Recipient need
TNCs	Trans-national corporations
UAE	United Arab Emirates
UK	United Kingdom
UN	United Nations
UNDP	United Nations Development Programme
UNICEF	United Nations Children's Fund
UNTA	United Nations Regular Programme of Technical Assistance
US	United States
WLS	Weighted least squares

1 Introduction

The aim of this book is to explain the pattern of aid giving in the 1990s by all the major donors with particular emphasis on the role of good governance (GG). GG comprises such things as democracy, respect for human rights, non-excessive military expenditures and the general quality of public sector management. The book's original contribution to the otherwise voluminous aid allocation literature is founded on three grounds. First, it looks at all the major aid donors, not merely one or a small selection of donors. Second, in addressing aid allocation in the period 1991–2000 it analyses more recent flows of aid than most other studies do. Third, and most importantly, this is the first study to comprehensively analyse whether aspects of GG have had an impact upon the allocation of aid.

Why focus on GG in an analysis of the pattern of aid giving in the 1990s? The reason is that one might expect GG to play a more important role in aid allocation in the 1990s than before. First, the end of the Cold War opened the way for putting less emphasis on promoting political and military-strategic interests in aid allocation and more emphasis on aspects of GG. The infamous Cold War saying 'We know they are bastards, but at least they are our bastards, not theirs', which justified much support to Cold War allies in spite of a bad governance record, fell out of fashion with the fall of the Berlin Wall. Second, the 1990s are not only characterised by greater opportunities to let GG impact upon aid allocation, but almost all (bilateral) donors organised in the Organisation for Economic Cooperation and Development's Development Assistance Committee (OECD-DAC) explicitly pledged to put greater emphasis on GG. The year 1990 saw representatives of such diverse governments as the Republican George Bush senior administration in the US, the conservative Thatcher and Kohl governments in the UK and Germany as well as the socialist government in France call for greater emphasis on democracy, human rights and other aspects of GG.

Chapter 2 describes in more detail this commitment of donors. It also argues why GG matters and analyses various strategies open to donors for improving governance in recipient countries. These include the persuasion, capacity building, conditionality and selectivity strategy. Of these, the selectivity strategy is the most important one in this context: Do donors select countries with GG with greater probability as eligible for aid and do they provide more aid to these countries than others? This will comprise the heart of this book's analysis.

Chapter 3 puts the analysis into perspective and context in providing an overview of existing studies. We will see that whilst there are many studies looking at individual donors, mainly the US, there are few comparative studies and even fewer with a particular focus on GG. It will become clear that there is a definite gap in the otherwise voluminous literature on aid allocation, which this book attempts to fill.

Chapter 4 lays down the research design for the analysis. As the backbone of this book consists of an econometric analysis of aid giving, it is necessary to justify the estimation methodology. This chapter describes which estimation techniques are used and why. One of the problems one faces in analysing the pattern of aid giving is that for some donors the percentage of potential recipient countries not receiving any actual positive amount of aid can be substantial. This clustering of observations at 'zero aid' causes some statistical problems, for which various estimation techniques are suitable. This chapter will analyse the Tobit, Heckman and the two-part model and justify why the last one is prefered. In this model, there are two stages – the aid eligibility stage, in which it is decided whether a potential recipient country receives any aid at all, and the level stage, in which it is decided how much aid to allocate to countries, which have been selected as eligible in the first stage. Furthermore, our data set has observations on the same countries over time. It consists of what is called panel data, for which special estimation techniques are also discussed in this chapter. What is called a random effects estimator has been used since many of the explanatory variables are time-invariant, for which this estimator is particularly suitable. Chapter 4 also defines in detail what is aid, the dependent variable. Such a definition is less straightforward than one might think as there exist various ways to operationalise it. What the OECD calls official development assistance (ODA) as well as official assistance (OA) is called aid in this book. OA is basically ODA to the so-called countries in transition in Eastern Europe and the republics of the former Soviet Union in Eastern Europe and Central Asia that are now independent countries. In this book, OA is included under the heading ODA so that ODA encompasses all aid. ODA comprises grants and loans with a grant element of at least 25 per cent. The dependent variable will be ODA to a recipient country as a share of the total aid allocated by a specific donor. Chapter 4 explains why such an operational definition is regarded as better than a definition of ODA in per capita terms. As a next step, the explanatory variables are described and justified. It is customary in the literature to model the allocation of aid as being influenced by both altruistic (recipient need, RN) and selfish (donor interest, DI) motivations. To these two groups of explanatory variables a third one is added, namely GG, which is the special focus of this book. Lastly, Chapter 4 discusses the specification of models to be tested.

The actual analysis begins with aggregate aid flows in Chapter 5. Bilateral aid is about twice as big as multilateral aid. Bilateral aid flows account for 68.4 per cent of total aid. Of these aid flows, finance provided by DAC countries makes up more than 96 per cent (see Table 1.1). Multilateral aid is, therefore, less than one-third of total aid flows. In addition, a large part of this aid stems from the European Community (EC), which is of course financed by its member states. Similarly, most of the finance for the other multilateral agencies derives from Western donors. Aid is, therefore, predominantly a business of Western donors giving aid to developing countries and countries in transition (Eastern European and Central Asian countries).

In addition to aggregate aid flows, individual donors are also looked at. Obviously, due to limitations of space not every single donor can be looked at, but aid giving by the biggest donors in the world is analysed: The big bilateral donors such as Japan, the US, Germany, France, Italy and the UK, the so-called like-minded countries Canada, Denmark, Norway, the Netherlands and Sweden, the Arab donors as well as the three major multilateral donors: the United Nations (UN), the EC and the World Bank's International Development Association (IDA).

After addressing aggregate aid flows, Chapter 5 goes on analysing the allocation of aid by the big bilateral aid donors. That these countries are called 'big aid donors' is entirely due to the size of their economy, not because they were such generous donors. Indeed, it can be seen from Table 1.2 that France, Germany, Italy, Japan, the UK and the US are average at best in their generosity to give aid as measured by total net ODA as a percentage of the donor's gross national income (GNI). Nevertheless, the sheer amount of money allocated by these countries is enormous. Table 1.1 presents the total amount in current dollars as well as the percentage of total aid volumes in the period 1991–2000, which can be attributed to specific donors. Note that the information contained in this table needs to be treated with care. First, it does not include aid, which cannot be traced back to individual recipient countries. Second and more importantly, for country donors it includes only aid bilaterally allocated, not aid allocated via multilateral sources. That Japan's aid is so much higher than US aid is partly to be explained by the fact that the US channels more of its aid through multilateral agencies than Japan does.

Chapter 5 also addresses the allocation of aid by the like-minded countries. This group comprises Canada, Denmark, the Netherlands, Norway and

Table 1.1 Net ODA (current US$)

	1991–2000	*Percentage of total*
The big Western donors		
EC	57,345	8.45
Germany	54,864	8.09
France	49,002	7.22
Italy	16,012	2.36
Japan	154,399	22.76
UK	18,486	2.72
US	79,755	11.76
The like-minded countries		
Canada	8,993	1.33
Denmark	6,975	1.03
The Netherlands	15,286	2.25
Norway	6,986	1.03
Sweden	7,851	1.16
Other Western donors		
Australia	7,644	1.13
Austria	6,347	0.94
Belgium	3,778	0.56
Finland	2,407	0.35
Ireland	735	0.11
Luxembourg	541	0.08
New Zealand	509	0.07
Portugal	1,784	0.26
Spain	8,051	1.19
Switzerland	5,576	0.82
Arab donors		
Arab countries	12,740	1.88
Arab agencies	3,310	0.49
Development Banks		
IDA	81,027	11.94
African Development Bank	6,001	0.88
Asian Development Bank	19,770	2.91
Inter-American Development Bank	5,735	0.85
United Nations agencies		
UNDP	6,166	0.91
UNICEF	6,488	0.96
UNTA	2,518	0.39
Total UN agencies	34,231	5.05
Total DAC	447,216	65.9
Bilateral total	464,100	68.4
Multilateral total	214,305	31.6
Total	678,405	100

Source: OECD (2002a).

Table 1.2 Net ODA from DAC countries as a percentage
of GNI (average 1991–2000)

	Percentage of GNI
The big donors	
Germany	0.32
France	0.51
Italy	0.22
Japan	0.28
UK	0.29
US	0.13
The like-minded countries	
Canada	0.37
Denmark	1.01
The Netherlands	0.82
Norway	0.95
Sweden	0.85
Others	
Australia	0.31
Austria	0.28
Belgium	0.36
Finland	0.42
Greece	0.16
Ireland	0.26
Luxembourg	0.47
New Zealand	0.25
Portugal	0.27
Spain	0.25
Switzerland	0.35
Total DAC	0.27
EU members	0.38

Source: OECD (2002a).

Sweden. These countries are commonly put into one group as they share a certain philosophy of aid giving. Traditionally, their aid is directed towards poverty alleviation (Stokke 1989). As seen in Chapter 2, the like-minded countries are also those that have put most emphasis on aspects of GG, in particular democracy and human rights. With the notable exception of Canada, the like-minded countries are also the most generous of the Western donors and the only ones whose ODA to GNI ratio exceeds the 0.7 per cent threshold, recommended by the UN and in principle, but not in practice, accepted by Western donors (see Table 1.2).

Finally, Chapter 5 looks at the biggest of the multilateral agencies: the UN agencies, the EC and the World Bank's IDA. The IDA accounts for about 12 per cent of the aid flows in the study, the EC for another 8.5 per cent. In comparison, the amount of aid going through UN agencies is relatively small at 5 per cent.

Chapter 6 addresses aid provided by Arab countries, both bilaterally as well as channelled through multilateral Arab organisations.[1] Arab countries are not the only donors of aid other than the Western countries organised in the OECD's DAC, but they are the only major ones. Other donors such as Iceland, Turkey, the Czech Republic, India, South Korea, China and Taiwan provide only very small amounts and, with the exception of Iceland, are recipients of aid flows themselves. Having said this, the Arab donors account for less than 2.4 per cent of the total aid flows, which is small compared to the DAC countries, which provide almost 66 per cent of the total aid flows bilaterally and a great part of the rest via multilateral agencies. One needs to keep in mind, of course, that Arab donors are fewer than the OECD donors and that their total income is much smaller than the combined total income of their Western counterparts.

Chapter 7 provides an analysis and discussion of the results, which were merely reported in Chapters 5 and 6. A comparison is made of the impact of various variables upon the allocation of aid across donors at both the aid eligibility and the level stage. Also, in addition to the statistical significance of variables, their substantive importance are compared as well. It will be seen that the variables of GG are of both limited statistical significance and limited substantive importance in the allocation of aid in the 1990s by most donors.

Chapter 8 checks the robustness of our results with respect to changes in model specification. It also deals with a problem that has been neglected up to then. A recipient country's income level and exports of goods and services from the donor to the recipient country are two of the explanatory variables we will use for explaining the pattern of aid giving. There are good reasons to presume, however, that income and exports are in turn also affected by the amount of aid given. After all, to raise income levels in recipient countries is one of the main objectives of aid and it is no secret either that often donors promote their own exports with their aid. Statistically speaking, this feedback mechanism creates the problem of so-called endogeneity of these explanatory variables. This problem is tackled with the help of so-called instrumental variables, the rationale of which is explained in this chapter. It will be seen that the results are not much affected.

Chapter 9 provides a summary of results and conclusions from the analysis. Readers who would like to jump to the results first might want to start with this chapter.

Before the analysis starts, a few words regarding its limitations. Explaining the pattern of aid giving is a mainly positive exercise. In particular, the analysis differs from normative approaches, which try to postulate criteria according to which aid should be allocated and evaluate actual aid giving according to these criteria. As examples of such studies the reader will find useful McGillivray (1989), Clark (1992), White and McGillivray (1995), Rao (1997), Collier and Dollar (1999) and Llavador and Roemer (2001). Neither does this book analyse why some donors give more aid in absolute terms than others and why the volume of these absolute aid flows changes over time. On these aspects of aid giving, see, for example, Lumsdaine (1993), Noël and Thérien (1995) and Hopkins (2002). In this book, I take the overall amount of aid as given and am merely interested in how the total cake is divided amongst all potential recipient countries. As will be seen, this already represents a formidable task.

2 Good governance and its relation to aid

Good governance defined

The term 'good governance' (GG) is sometimes rather narrowly defined in terms of public sector management with, for example, democracy and respect for human rights being seen as additional to GG. This book takes a broad and comprehensive view of GG instead. Governance is defined as the way in which policy makers are empowered to make decisions, the way in which policy decisions are formulated and implemented and the extent to which governmental intervention is allowed to encroach into the rights of citizens. GG respects the political, civil and human rights of citizens, is in accordance with the rule of law, provides effective and non-corrupted public services to the people and utilises public resources in an accountable and transparent way and with the aim of promoting the general social welfare.

Why good governance matters

Why be concerned about GG? The most fundamental reason is that GG is a worthy goal to achieve in and of itself. All human beings should have guaranteed political, civil and human rights in order to live a fulfilled life. Respect for the rule of law provides citizens with confidence and trust in the judiciary system and shields them from arbitrary discretion and encroachments into their rights. Competent and non-corrupt provision of public services means that people receive good value for their tax money and do not need to bribe officials to get access to public services. Keeping military expenditures low frees financial resources to be spent on more productive purposes aimed at promoting the social welfare such as education, health and other social services. Those who are responsible for bad governance are guilty of depriving their people from living a more empowered, secure, confident, dignified and meaningful human life.

In addition to this fundamental justification, GG, or at least aspects of it, might also be of instrumental value, particularly in the context of aid giving, the subject of the present analysis. There has been a great debate in recent years about the hypothesis that the effectiveness of aid giving might depend on the quality of governance, where effectiveness is perhaps somewhat narrowly defined as raising the economic growth rate relative to the situation without aid inflows. A World Bank (1998) report called *Assessing Aid: What Works, What Doesn't, and Why* created a lot of attention and sparked much dispute with its proposition that aid is only truly effective in countries with sound economic policies and GG, but is typically ineffective in countries with highly distortive economic policies and bad governance. This report took a rather narrow view of governance, which refers to respect for the rule of law, the quality of the public bureaucracy and the pervasiveness of corruption. Sound economic policy is interpreted as keeping the country open to trade, inflation rates and budget deficits low. In later research, a somewhat broader and more comprehensive view of what constitutes sound economic policy was taken. The policy implication drawn from the World Bank report is that aid can be made much more effective and more people taken out of poverty if more aid is given to countries with sound economic policies and GG.

The report itself and the major research on which the report was based as well as later similar work undertaken by World Bank staff soon came under fierce attack. For example, Lensink and White (2000a,b), Hansen and Tarp (2000, 2001) and Dalgard and Hansen (2001) all attack the econometric analyses underlying the writings by Burnside and Dollar (1997, 2000), Collier and Dollar (1999, 2001) and World Bank (1998), mainly on methodological grounds. The critics argue that there is no conclusive systematic econometric evidence that aid is ineffective in terms of raising the economic growth rate unless sound economic policies and GG in the sense of the World Bank definition are in place. I do not want to engage in this ongoing dispute here. Indeed, I will not even take sides. Instead, it is merely noted that if the proposition of the World Bank and its staff is correct, then there is an additional reason for donors to be concerned about certain aspects of the quality of governance in recipient countries and an additional incentive to try to improve it. But it should be noted that the World Bank's proposition, even if valid, relates only to certain aspects of GG and that GG in its more comprehensive definition is entirely desirable in and of itself and not dependent on the validity of the Bank's proposition.

Donors' commitment to good governance

Looking at what donors say and pledge, one might expect GG to play an important role in aid giving. For example, a document called 'DAC Orientations on Participatory Development and Good Governance', formally endorsed by the DAC at its High Level Meeting in December 1993, states the following:

> It has become increasingly apparent that there is a vital connection between open, democratic and accountable systems of governance and respect for human rights, and the ability to achieve sustained economic and social development. (...) This connection is so fundamental that participatory development and good governance must be central concerns in the allocation and design of development assistance.
>
> (OECD-DAC 1994: 7)

Selbervik (1997: 7) notes a 'wave of policy announcements by Western donors' in the 1990s postulating that GG 'will occupy a central place on the aid agenda'. Which aspects of GG are regarded as more important obviously depends somewhat on the particular donor. There seems to be a general agreement on what constitutes the most fundamental aspects of GG, however. The 'DAC Orientations on Participatory Development and Good Governance', for example, explicitly mentions political freedom and democracy, human rights, the rule of law, the quality of public sector management, the control of corruption and the reduction of 'excessive' military expenditures (OECD-DAC 1994). The European Council of Ministers similarly enumerated democracy, respect for human rights and the rule of law, effective and accountable public sector management, low corruption and non-excessive military expenditures in its resolution on 'Human Rights, Democracy and Development' from November 1991 (EU Council of Ministers 1991). The EC claims that it uses these as part of the criteria according to which countries in Africa, the Caribbean and the Pacific with historic links to the EC (so-called ACP countries) are allocated aid within the framework of its Lomé Convention (now: Cotonou Agreement). Bilateral donors also publicly embraced a similar list of aspects of GG in the 1990s. To provide some examples:

- For the UK, then Minister for Overseas Development, Baroness Chalker, listed the promotion of sound economic and social policies, the competence of government, democracy, respect for human rights and the rule of law as the essential aspects of GG in a speech held in June 1991 (Crawford 2000: 60).
- Japan, which had traditionally pursued mainly its own political and in particular economic interest (Ensign 1992; Arase 1995) and was regularly accused of being entirely insensitive to human rights issues (Tomaševski 1997: 31), passed a Foreign Aid Charter in 1992, which puts emphasis on democracy, human rights and low military expenditures as

important aspects of GG to influence its aid allocation (Japan MOFA 1992).

- Germany in 1991 listed respect for political freedom and human rights, rule of law, market-friendly economic policies and non-excessive military expenditures among its criteria of GG to impact upon its aid programme (Tomaševski 1997: 29).
- Sweden, which had traditionally put emphasis on democratic development in its aid programme, explicitly added respect for human rights and good public sector management as goals of its programme in the 1990s (Crawford 2000).

As concerns democracy and respect for human rights in particular, of all donors the so-called like-minded countries (Canada, Denmark, Norway, the Netherlands and Sweden) and the European Union (EU) have been most explicit in putting emphasis on the role of these aspects of GG (Selbervik 1997). In Norway, for example, respect for human rights traditionally played some role in the aid programme. As far back as 1984, a White Paper threatened aid cut-offs to countries whose government 'takes part in, tolerates or directly executes violations of human rights' (cited in Tomaševski 1997: 24). In Canada, respect for human rights gained importance in 1987 with a new aid strategy stating that 'in countries where violations of human rights are systematic, gross and continuous, and where it cannot be ensured that Canadian assistance reaches the people for whom it is intended, government-to-government (bilateral) aid will be reduced or denied', whereas countries with a good record can expect to receive more aid (cited in Keenleyside and Serkasevich 1989: 139). The EU incorporated a human rights clause into its fourth Lomé Convention and from 1995 onwards threatened to reduce or suspend cooperation with any ACP country guilty of violation of human rights.

How donors can assist good governance in recipient countries

If donor countries want to achieve improvements in governance in recipient countries, then they have a number of strategies available. First, donors might use their formal and informal contacts with recipient countries to persuade them into giving up their resistance and improve their governance. This is called the persuasion strategy. Second, donors might channel some of the aid into projects whose objective is to build up the capacity for GG. This is called the capacity-building strategy. Third, donors can impose conditions on the aid that countries receive to the effect that they reform their policies and succumb to specified criteria of GG. This is called the conditionality strategy. Fourth, donors can try to allocate non-conditional aid such as to reward countries with a proven past record of GG and punish those with bad governance. This is called the selectivity strategy.

The *persuasion strategy* is the least intrusive, but in many cases it is also the least effective. Bad governance exists for many reasons, but in most cases those in power have vested interests in keeping up the system of bad governance. This could be because they do not want to expose themselves to public critique and the risk of losing at the ballot box, which is why they suppress political, civil and human rights. Often they benefit from corruption in the provision of public services and discretion over the judiciary system that goes against the rule of law. They might have an interest in maintaining excessive military expenditures because they are militaries themselves or depend on militaries or they benefit from fuelling ongoing conflicts, be they internal or external. In all these and many more cases, the mere exercise of persuasion will not make much difference.

The *capacity-building strategy* has much in its favour. In particular, where bad governance is the consequence of lacking capacity rather than lack of will, this strategy might be most effective in bringing about positive changes. Of course, certain aspects of governance are more dependent on the good will of those in power than on their capacity. This is true, for example, with respect to political, civil and human rights. Even then, however, improvements in these aspects of governance sometimes depend on specific projects to be implemented that can be costly. Other aspects of GG, such as the quality of public sector management, are much more dependent on having the capacity of the public sector to provide good services in addition to the good will of the ruling elites. In all these cases, the capacity-building strategy represents an important ingredient of a donor's strategy to improve governance in recipient countries. Donors do not seem to do enough in this regard. Crawford (2000) has estimated that in the case of aid programmes in the early 1990s by the EU, the UK and the US less than 5 per cent of aid allocated could possibly be regarded as directed towards promoting GG (10 per cent in the case of Sweden). Gillies (1999: 242f.) praises the efforts of the Netherlands and Norway to promote human rights and democracy, but the reported figures are also very small compared to overall Dutch and Norwegian aid. Selbervik (1997: 43) comes to similar pessimistic conclusions for the case of capacity-building for democracy and human rights protection by the like-minded countries, which have traditionally put emphasis on these aspects of GG. He notes that 'the volume of aid going to this area is relatively modest and not commensurate with the high priority accorded to this sector in political statements'. Donors could, therefore, do much more to finance projects whose objective is to build up capacity for GG. One should not forget, however, that capacity-building can only be effective where it is matched by support of the ruling elites of the

recipient countries. For the many cases, where those in power systematically benefit from bad governance (as argued above), neither persuasion
nor capacity-building are likely to be effective tools for bringing about
improvements in governance. In these cases, the remaining two strategies
are potentially more effective since they are based on the exercise of power
of donors over recipient countries.

The *conditionality strategy* is problematic for a range of reasons, however.
First, it interferes substantially with the sovereignty of the recipient country
and is, therefore, bound to be met with the same kind of hostility as conditionality of the International Monetary Fund (IMF) for its structural adjust-
ment programmes. The intrusiveness of stringent conditionality has not only
been criticised from left-wing analysts and activists, but also from conservative economists such as Martin Feldstein (Singh 2002). Those who want
to resist conditionality find it easy to gather support behind them against the
external imposition of conditions even though the very same conditions
might be in the (long-term) interest of the people. As Dijkstra (2002: 310)
argues, it is an inherent contradiction of comprehensive conditionality that it
necessarily clashes with democratic decision-making within the country,
whilst moving towards democratisation ironically is sometimes one of the
conditions imposed. It also clashes with the concept of local ownership of
the reform process as the process does not originate from a domestic desire
to reform, but is externally imposed via conditions (Collier 1997).

Second, recipient countries will do their best to merely create the image
of compliance with the conditions imposed and revert to their old policies
as soon as the donors turn away their attention. Ironically, this sometimes
has the perverse consequence that the same reform is sold several times to
donors eager to allocate aid on the condition of reform, but unwilling or
unable to withhold the funds if the reform is not implemented (Collier
1997). In principle, promised or at least future funds could be revoked once
the cheating becomes detected, but, as Allen and Weinhold (2000: 861)
observe for the case of IMF and World Bank lending, it is very difficult to
withhold funds ex post if recipient countries do not comply (fully) with the
ex ante agreed upon conditionality. If non-compliance is only partial, there
is always the incentive to ignore it so as not to endanger the whole programme (Collier 1997). Also, donors are constrained in their decision-
making by other interests, which stand against withholding funds. This
leads to erratic and inconsistent treatment of those who violate or ignore
conditions imposed, which undermines the credibility of the donors
themselves (Tomaševski 1997; Killick 1998; Crawford 2000; Kanbur 2000).
Furthermore, the executing aid agencies might have incentives to maximise
the amount of aid disbursed and might, therefore, shy away from withholding
funds (Leandro *et al.* 1999; Svensson 2003).

Third, reforms towards improving governance are hard work and often linked with short-term costs and painful adjustments to influential lobby groups. Paradoxically, aid, even conditional aid, can reduce the very incentives for reform as it takes away some of the pressure from policy makers to improve governance in order to enhance the long-term welfare of their country (Dijkstra 2002). Fourth, it is doubtful at least whether GG can be externally imposed via conditions. Bad governance is usually deeply entrenched in a country's political system with those in power benefiting systematically from bad governance. It can only be overcome slowly and with the full support of the governing elites. In her assessment of aid conditionality in eight developing countries, Dijkstra (2002: 331) comes to the conclusion that 'demands with respect to the political system were not honoured in any country, and whilst donors may have some influence in the fight against corruption, this happens only if corruption is also seen as a domestic issue'. Fifth, for the reasons just mentioned conditionality often does not and cannot tackle the root causes of bad governance and is usually instead targeted at easily observable aspects of governance such as macroeconomic stabilisation policies that do not require further structural or institutional changes in the governance system (Leando *et al.* 1999).[1]

The conditionality strategy is, therefore, problematic on various accounts. Hence, the *selectivity strategy* remains. It wants to give more aid to countries with a demonstrated record of GG with the hope that in rewarding GG these countries will strive to maintain GG in the future and other countries with bad governance will perceive it necessary to improve their governance in order to receive higher aid flows. The World Bank has recently become a vocal proponent of this strategy – witness its 1998 report on aid effectiveness (World Bank 1998). The selectivity strategy suspects that bad governance is mainly due to those in power systematically benefiting from bad governance. Hence, it sees little point in rewarding the beneficiaries of bad governance with aid flows, which would only prolong and cement the system of bad governance. Bräutigam (2000) finds evidence that large aid inflows into countries with bad governance provide a disincentive for the ruling elite to try to improve the quality of governance: 'High levels of aid in countries where the political leadership does not have reform on the agenda are likely to reduce the incentive to cooperate in the sacrifices necessary for reform to occur. Instead, aid becomes part of the system of patronage and political survival'. The much debated World Bank (1998: 3) report on aid effectiveness mentioned above comes to a similar conclusion: 'Efforts to "buy" policy improvements in countries where there is no movement for reform (…) have typically failed'.

Instead, the selectivity strategy wants to send out a clear signal that those who are willing to establish a system of GG are rewarded with higher aid flows, whereas those who are not will have to do with low aid flows, if any.

Collier (1997: 75) hopes that 'by creating star performers, selectivity would induce many non-reforming governments to change their policies through the pressure of emulation'. As it conditions aid on a demonstrated record of GG it is not dependent on the promises of policy makers in recipient countries, which can easily be reneged upon, but on their revealed policy choices.

Western donors have at various points pledged not to shy away from reducing volumes of aid and excluding countries from the receipt of aid altogether if these countries exhibit a very bad performance in governance (EU Council of Ministers 1991; OECD-DAC 1994: 9, 23; Crawford 2000). Perhaps no other country has made this more explicit than the Netherlands, which described the link between GG and aid allocation in a policy document on Africa from 2001 as follows (Dutch Ministry of Foreign Affairs 2001):

> The Dutch activities to support good governance call for a careful selection of partner countries, counterparts and programmes. A condensed list of countries was recently approved by parliament. We feel that good governance must be rewarded, partly because it will make aid more effective. The emphasis is on poor countries which have demonstrated over the longer term that they are serious about good governance, essential elements of which are respect for human rights and an independent judiciary.

The selectivity strategy might also help to overcome the so-called aid fatigue in many donor countries, where support for aid programmes among policy makers and voters has been dwindling. Voters are more likely to support aid giving if such aid does not go to undemocratic, human rights abusing and badly governed countries. Note that this is likely to remain true even if the impetus to improve the quality of governance following a reduction of aid to countries with bad governance might be small because voters simply do not want to see their money going to such regimes.

Which strategy to choose?

In my own view, the selectivity strategy accompanied by the capacity-building strategy are the best avenues for donors who intend to achieve improvements in governance in recipient countries. I would like to stress the importance of accompanying measures to build up the capacity for GG. Where recipient countries show clear willingness to improve the quality of their governance, but lack the capacity to do so, they should be supported with higher levels of general aid as well as specific aid for capacity building even though the quality of governance is still poor. Such a more flexible approach would somewhat relieve the concern of those who believe with Pronk (2001) that a rigid selectivity strategy might leave helpless those most in need of help. The literature advocating the selectivity strategy sometimes fails to distinguish enough between countries where bad governance is the consequence of lack of will and others where bad governance is more the consequence of lacking capacity.

Of course, the selectivity strategy is not free from problems either. For example, it is still indirectly intrusive as a country has to fulfil certain conditions for being selected to receive any aid at all or higher flows of aid, but it is much less so than the conditionality strategy. If donors fail to act consistently and apply selectivity erratically, then they undermine their credibility and hence the credibility of the selectivity strategy. There is much evidence that conditionality is applied inconsistently in that donors are tough with weak states (such as Malawi) and pariah states (such as Myanmar), but not with those in which they have major commercial or other interests (such as China) (Gillies 1999). If selectivity were to be applied similarly inconsistently, it would lose much of its appeal. Furthermore, if countries under a regime of bad governance are punished with reductions in aid flows then poor and vulnerable people might suffer from these reductions who are entirely innocent. Of course, it is questionable whether aid flows to countries with bad governance reach these people anyway, but donors might maintain certain forms of mainly humanitarian aid in spite of poor governance. They should then try to bypass governmental authorities as far as possible and work together with private and non-governmental organisations.

But, whatever are the merits of each strategy for improving governance in recipient countries, in the end the selectivity strategy is the only one amenable to quantitative testing in the framework of our analysis. The exercise of persuasion via formal and informal contacts is often not publicly known and even where it is known, it is not quantifiable. The financial flows put into capacity building are in principle quantifiable, but data are far too sparse to go beyond a case based study as undertaken by, for example, Selbervik (1997) and Crawford (2000). Information on conditions imposed on aid flows are similarly difficult to get hold of and would be difficult to quantify. The selectivity strategy, on the other hand, is relatively easy to test in comparison. In this book, therefore, it is to be systematically tested whether there is evidence that donors have used the selectivity strategy. If evidence is not found, it is not to be automatically concluded that the pledge to put emphasis on GG amounts to no more than empty words. After all, donors could still try to achieve improvements in governance in recipient countries through other channels. But in the light of the preceding points, failure to find such evidence would in all fairness provide a *prima facie* case against the sincerity of donors' commitment to promote GG in their aid programmes. Note that emphasis on GG does not imply that it represents the only or even the major criterion for aid allocation. Indeed, in the next chapter we will see that the existing literature mainly explains aid allocation in terms of donor interest and recipient need. It is merely tested if, after controlling for all sorts of aspects of donor interest and recipient need, GG has at least a statistically significant, if perhaps substantively small, impact upon the pattern of aid allocation. Given that donors typically do not give aid to all countries, does GG raise the likelihood of being eligible for the receipt of aid, all other things equal? Given that donors allocate vastly differing amounts of aid to eligible countries, does GG imply higher aid flows, all other things equal? These two questions are at the centre of the analysis.

3 Overview of existing studies

Donor interest, recipient need and good governance

Ever since McKinlay and Little (1977, 1978a,b,c, 1979) in a series of articles analysed aid allocation by Germany, France, the UK and the US, it has become common in the literature explaining aid allocation to distinguish between variables that control for donor interest (DI) versus recipient need (RN). The simple idea behind this distinction is that donors are likely to be neither entirely altruistic, which is why their aid allocation can be expected to promote their own interest, nor entirely selfish, which is why it can also be expected to be oriented towards the need for aid of recipient countries. This is not to say that McKinlay and Little were the first ones to include such variables in a quantitative analysis of aid allocation, but they can be credited with providing a logical framework to this type of analysis with the help of such categories. Note that the proposition that donor countries promote partially at least their own interest fits well into the realist school of thought within international relations, whereas the idea that donor countries are concerned about the need within recipient countries is rooted in the idealist school of thought of international relations.

What is less commonly paid attention to is that McKinlay and Little already also tested for the role of what they called 'political stability and democracy' on aid allocation and what would later become known as aspects of GG. Perhaps not surprisingly then, whilst most studies following McKinlay and Little's work included variables of DI and RN in one way or another in their analysis, only some also tested for aspects of GG, which has only recently become a major focus of interest again.

Donor interest

McKinlay and Little had already included a long and complex list of various aspects of DI in their work and it is difficult to find two studies by different authors that would include exactly the same variables. Partly this is due to the fact that DI is a vague concept that can be given differing interpretations and partly due to the desire of researchers to do things slightly differently from the existing literature. Having said this, most studies try to control for one or more of the following: political, economic, military-strategic and cultural interests of donors. Not surprisingly, which aspect is stressed and how it is made operational depends a bit on the time period studied and the specific donor looked at as well. For example, it is not surprising that during the Cold War period military-strategic aspects played an important role.

Recipient need

Whilst a variety of variables are also used to test for the role of RN on aid allocation, the single variable most often included is per capita income. The simple idea is that the poorer a country, usually measured as gross domestic product (GDP) or gross national product (GNP) per capita, the more it is in need of aid. Early studies used income data at official exchange rates. With the availability of purchasing power parity (PPP) estimates it became, later on, a standard to use income data at PPP, which reflects more adequately the true power of incomes to purchase goods and services. Apart from income, other variables sometimes included fall into either one of two categories: first, either they attempt to broaden the concept of poverty in including aspects of human development need that are strongly correlated, but still conceptually different from income – infant mortality, literacy, life expectancy, malnutrition and the like. Second, some studies sought to include other aspects of economic need not directly captured by per capita income by including variables such as the foreign reserve position, the current account balance, the external debt position, the government budget, the inflation rate and the like.

Donor interest or recipient need? or both?

It would be vastly beyond the scope of this book to provide a detailed review and critique of the dozens of studies that have analysed aid allocation by donors with the help of multivariate regression analysis. An overview of those studies is given in Table 3.1. It is sorted alphabetically by the author and lists which donor is looked at over what time period, which estimation technique is used and how the dependent variable is defined. It groups the explanatory variables used into either DI, RN, GG or others. Note that the allocation of variables into one of these groups is my own one, which can at times clash with what the authors suggest. For example, Schraeder *et al.* (1998) consider GNP per capita to be a variable of DI as a proxy of economic potential. While such an interpretation is perhaps possible, even though total GNP rather than GNP per capita might make more sense as a proxy for economic potential, I have grouped GNP per capita under RN, which is the standard procedure in the literature. In the last column, a short summary of the major findings of each study is given, mainly with respect to whether supporting evidence for the DI, RN or GG variables was found and whether a bias towards less populous and middle-income countries is apparent. (See further below on why these biases might exist in the allocation of aid.) Also note that whilst this overview encompasses all studies we know of, it is not pretended that it covers all existing analyses. In particular, there will exist earlier studies as well as studies in other languages than English that are not listed in Table 3.1.

Given that no comprehensive review and critique of individual studies can be given here, a few general conclusions are presented that survive the often conflicting results, which are the consequence of different research design such as different periods of study, different dependent and independent variables, different estimation techniques and the like. Maybe not surprisingly, there is evidence that both DI *and* RN play some role in the aid allocation by most donors. In other words, the expectation that donors are neither entirely selfish nor entirely altruistic is confirmed by the available evidence. The relative importance of DI versus RN depends on the donor looked at. At the risk of oversimplification, it is probably fair to say that the majority of the evidence seems to suggest that RN is more important at the aggregate multilateral level as well as for individual multilateral donors, whereas DI is more important at the aggregate bilateral level as well as for many, but not all, individual bilateral donors. As concerns the latter, at one extreme are bilateral donors like France for which DI clearly seems to dominate aid allocation and at the other extreme the like-minded countries (Canada, Denmark, Norway and the Netherlands), which have traditionally put much emphasis on recipients' needs in their aid giving.

Good governance

As mentioned above, greater interest in the effect of GG on aid allocation is of a more recent nature. Right from the start political and civil rights, often subsumed under the heading democracy, played a prominent role. These rights typically refer to things like the freedom to organise in political parties or groupings, the existence of elections and an effective opposition that has the possibility to take over power via those elections, freedom of expression, freedom of the media, freedom of assembly, prevalence of the rule of law and the like. Later on the focus on human rights was broadened and perhaps sharpened in that so-called personal integrity rights were additionally included. Personal integrity rights, sometimes also called physical integrity or life integrity rights, refer to things like freedom from political imprisonment, torture, disappearance, violence and political murder. Very recent is a focus on GG defined more comprehensively, where aspects such as the extent of corruption, respect for the rule of law, non-excessive military expenditures and the like have been looked at.

Table 3.1 An overview of multivariate regression studies on the determinants of aid allocation

Study and donor looked at	Period of study	Estimation technique	Explained variable	Donor interest (DI) variables	Recipient need (RN) variables	Good governance (GG) variables	Other variables	Main findings
Abrams and Lewis (1991): US	1989, cross-sectional	Tobit	Aid p.c.	Regional and country dummies % White % Christian	GDP p.c.	Human rights index		Support for DI, RN and GG
Alesina and Dollar (2000): various donors	1970–94, panel	OLS and Tobit	Aid p.c.	Colonial experience UN voting similarity Country dummies % Muslim % Roman Catholic	GDP p.c.	Political and civil rights Rule of law Trade openness	Population	Support for DI as major determinants, RN, political/ civil rights and trade openness for most donors
Alesina and Weder (2000): various donors	1970–95, panel	OLS and Tobit	Aid p.c.	Colonial experience UN voting similarity Country dummies	GDP p.c.	Political rights Corruption	Population	Only Scandinavian donors lumped together and Australia reward low levels of corruption
Anyadike-Danes and Anyadike-Danes (1992): EC	1975–88, panel	OLS	Total aid	Historical relationships with EC Regional and country dummies	GDP p.c. Least developed country dummy		Population	Support for RN and DI
Apodaca and Stohl (1999): US	1976–95, panel	Two-part model (Logit and fixed effects)	Military and economic aid p.c.	Exports Number of US military personnel in country Latin America dummy	GDP p.c.	Personal integrity rights	Lagged aid p.c. Dummy for Presidential Administrations	Support for RN at eligibility stage and for DI and GG at eligibility and level stages
Arvin and Drewes (2001): Germany	1973–95, panel	GLS	Aid p.c.	Exports ACP countries dummy	GDP p.c.		Population	Small population bias, but no middle-income bias

(continued)

Table 3.1 (Continued)

Study and donor looked at	Period of study	Estimation technique	Explained variable	Donor interest (DI) variables	Recipient need (RN) variables	Good governance (GG) variables	Other variables	Main findings
Bowles (1987): UK	1970–81, panel	OLS	Aid p.c.	Colonial experience Exports FDI stock	GNP p.c. Change in savings rate Change in terms of Trade Change in debt-service ratio Change in growth rate Life expectancy Population growth		Population Total aid Lagged aid received from other donors	Support for DI as major determinant and RN
Bowles (1989): EC	1975–81, panel	OLS	Aid p.c.	Colonial experience Exports FDI stock	GNP p.c. Growth rate Savings rate Change in savings rate Terms of Trade		Population Total aid Lagged aid received from other donors	Support for DI as major determinant and RN
Carleton and Stohl (1987): US	1982, cross-sectional	OLS	Total economic aid	Trade with US Trade with Soviet bloc Geopolitical importance dummy	Level of development Trade deficit	Political and civil rights Personal integrity rights	Population Multilateral aid Political instability	Sensitivity analysis of Cingranelli and Pasquarello (1985) finding little evidence for GG at level stage
Cingranelli and Pasquarello (1985): US	1982, cross-sectional	Two-part model (Logit and OLS)	Total economic and military aid	Trade with US Trade with Soviet bloc Geopolitical importance dummy	Level of development Trade deficit	Index of personal integrity, political and civil rights	Population Multilateral aid Political instability	Support for GG only at level stage for economicaid as major determinant

Study	Period, data	Method	Dependent variable	Independent variables	Income variables	Political variables	Other variables	Results
Davenport (1971): aggregate bilateral multilateral and US	1962–64, panel	OLS	Aid p.c. and aid per GNP		Income p.c. Foreign reserve position		Population FDI as % of GDP	Middle-income bias
Dowling and Hiemenz (1985): aggregate bilateral and multilateral	1970s, cross-sectional and panel	OLS	Aid p.c.		Income p.c.		Population	Small population bias, but no middle-income bias
Dudley and Montmarquette (1976): various donors	1970	Two-part model (Probit and OLS)	Aid p.c.	Colonial experience Exports Regional dummies	GNP p.c.		Population Aid from other donors	Support for DI and RN
Frey and Schneider (1986): World Bank and IDA	1972–81, cross-sectional and panel	OLS	Loans and aid p.c.	Capitalist dummy Colonial experience Exports	GNP p.c. Inflation rate Balance of payments Government budget deficit External debt	Political instability	Past growth	Support for DI and RN as well as bureaucratic self-interest of donors
Gang and Lehman (1990): US	1960–80, cross-sectional	OLS and Tobit	Aid as share of total aid	Exports	GDP p.c. Child mortality	Political instability		No consistent support for either model
Gounder (1994): Australia	1971–92, cross-sectional and panel	OLS	Aid p.c.	Exports Stock of FDI Regional and country dummies Military aid	GNP p.c. Growth rate Balance of payments			Support for DI and RN

(continued)

Table 3.1 (Continued)

Study and donor looked at	Period of study	Estimation technique	Explained variable	Donor interest (DI) variables	Recipient need (RN) variables	Good governance (GG) variables	Other variables	Main findings
Gounder and Doessel (1994): Australia	1986–92, cross-sectional	OLS	Aid p.c.	Exports Stock of FDI Regional and country dummies Military aid	GNP p.c. Growth rate Balance of payments		Population Lagged aid	Small population bias, but no middle-income bias
Gounder (1995): Australia	1986–92, cross-sectional and panel	OLS	Aid p.c.	Exports Stock of FDI Regional and country dummies Military aid	GNP p.c. Growth rate Balance of payments		Population Lagged aid	Support for DI and RN
Grilli and Riess (1992): EC	1971–88, cross-sectional	OLS	Aid p.c.	Exports	HDI External debt		Population	Support for DI as major determinant and RN for aggregate bilateral aid flows Support for RN as major determinants and DI for aggregate multilateral aid flows
Gulhati and Nallari (1988): various donors	1975–84, cross-sectional	OLS	Aid p.c.	Colonial experience Arms transfers Exports	GNP p.c. Balance of payments Terms of trade		Population	No consistent support for either model
Hout (2002): the Netherlands	2000, cross-sectional	Logit	Aid eligibility		GNP p.c.	Political and civil rights Political stability and lack of violence Government effectiveness Regulatory burden Rule of law Corruption		Support for RN No support for GG apart from partial support for regulatory burden

Isenman (1976): various donors	1969–74, cross-sectional	OLS	Aid p.c. and total aid	GNP p.c. Balance of payments		Population Numerous other variables	Small population bias and middle-income bias
Karunaratne (1980): Australia	1976, cross-sectional	OLS	Total aid	Exports Country dummies	GNP p.c. PQLI	Population	Small population bias and middle-income bias
Katada (1997): Japan	1971–91, panel	WLS	Total aid	Exports FDI Number of Japanese immigrants US exports US economic and military aid	GNP p.c.	Trade openness	Population	Support for DI as major determinant, RN and GG
McGillivray and Oczkowski (1991): Australia	1980–86, cross-sectional and panel	Sample selection	Total aid	Exports Regional and country dummies	GNP p.c. Least developed country dummy	Population	Support for DI and RN
McGillivray and Oczkowski (1992): UK	1980–87, cross-sectional and panel	Sample selection	Total aid	Arms transfers Exports Commonwealth dummy	GNP p.c. Least developed country dummy	Population Aid by other donors	Support for DI and RN
McKinlay and Little (1977, 1978a,b,c, 1979): France, Germany, US, UK	1960–70, cross-sectional	OLS	Aid p.c.	Numerous	Numerous	Political stability and democracy	Support for DI as major determinant and RN

(continued)

Table 3.1 (Continued)

Study and donor looked at	Period of study	Estimation technique	Explained variable	Donor interest (DI) variables	Recipient need (RN) variables	Good governance (GG) variables	Other variables	Main findings
Maizels and Nissanke (1984): various donors and aggregate bilateral and multilateral	1969–70 and 1978–80, cross-sectional	OLS	Aid p.c.	Arms transfers Stock of FDI Number of TNCs Regional dummies Strategic materials export dummy	GNP p.c. Growth rate PQLI Balance of payments		Population	Support for DI for bilateral donors; support for RN for multilateral aid flows
Neumayer (2003a): regional development banks, UN agencies and aggregate multilateral	1983–97, panel	OLS	Aid as share of total aid	Colonial experience Distance Security Interests	GDP p.c. PQLI	Political and civil rights Personal integrity rights Corruption	Population	Mixed support for DI and RN Very limited support for GG (confined to political and civil rights)
Neumayer (2003b): aggregate bilateral and multilateral	1984–95, panel	OLS	Aid (EDA) as share of total aid	Colonial experience Distance Egypt dummy Socialist dummy	GDP p.c.	Political and civil rights Personal integrity rights	Population	Support for DI, RN Inconsistent support for GG
Neumayer (2003c): 21 OECD donors	1985–97, panel	Two-part model (Probit and OLS)	Aid as share of total aid	Colonial experience Exports US military grants Distance	GDP p.c.	Political and civil rights Personal integrity rights	Population	Support for DI and RN for most donors Support for civil and political political rights at eligibility stage for most donors and at level stage for some donors

Study	Period	Model	Dependent variable	Independent variables		Human rights measure	Control variables	Results
Neumayer (2003d): Arab countries and agencies	1974–97, panel	Sample selection model	Aid as share of total aid	Exports UN voting similarity Arab dummy Sub-Saharan Africa dummy Islam dummy Diplomatic relations with Israel dummy Socialist dummy	GDP p.c.		Population Total aid	Support for personal integrity rights only in few cases at either stage No systematic difference between like-minded and other donors Support for DI as major determinant and RN
Payaslian (1996): US	1982–91, panel	Two-part model (Probit and OLS)	Total economic and military aid	Geopolitical interests Ideological orientation Trade	GNP p.c.	Index of personal integrity, political and civil rights	Press coverage of human rights abuses Bureaucratic variables Lagged aid	No confirmation for GG
Poe (1992): US	1980–84, cross-sectional	Two-part model (Probit and OLS)	Total economic aid	Strategic importance Ideological orientation dummy UN voting similarity Trade	GNP p.c.	Personal integrity rights	Population	Support for DI, RN and GG

(continued)

Table 3.1 (Continued)

Study and donor looked at	Period of study	Estimation technique	Explained variable	Donor interest (DI) variables	Recipient need (RN) variables	Good governance (GG) variables	Other variables	Main findings
Poe and Sirirangsi (1994): US	1983–88, cross-sectional	Two-part model (Probit and OLS)	Total economic aid	Central America dummy Communist border dummy Ideological orientation dummy Trade	GNP p.c.	Personal integrity rights	Population	Support for GG at eligibility stage, but not at level stage
Poe et al. (1994): US	1983–91, panel	GLS	Total economic and military aid	Central America and country dummies Ideological orientation dummy Land area US military presence dummy Trade	GNP p.c.	Index of civil, political and personal integrity rights	Population	Support for DI as major determinant and RN and GG
Schraeder et al. (1998): Japan, France, Sweden and US	1980–89, panel	GLS	Aid as % of GNP	Ideological orientation dummies Colonial experience Regional dummies Strategic importance	GNP p.c. Caloric intake Life expectancy		Lagged aid	Support for DI and RN
Svensson (1999): various donors	1970–95, panel	Two-part model (Probit and OLS)	Total aid and aid as % of GDP		GDP p.c.	Civil and political rights	Population	Support for GG for some donors

Study	Period, data	Method	Aid measure	Regional dummies / donor interest	GDP / need	Corruption	Population	Result
Svensson (2000): combined aggregate bilateral and multilateral	1980–94, panel	2SLS	Aid as % of GDP	Regional dummies	GDP p.c. Terms of trade	Corruption	Population	No support for GG
Trumbull and Wall (1994): combined aggregate bilateral and multilateral	1984–89, panel	Fixed and random effects	Aid p.c.		GNP p.c. Infant mortality	Civil and political rights	Population	Support for RN and GG
Tsoutsoplides (1991): EC	1975–80, cross-sectional	OLS	Aid p.c.	Exports Number of TNCs Strategic materials export dummy Colonial experience dummy Military interests	GDP p.c. Growth rate PQLI Balance of payments		Population	Support for RN as major determinant and DI
Wall (1995): aggregate aid	1979–80, 1984–85, 1988–89, cross-sectional	OLS	Aid p.c.		GNP p.c. Infant mortality	Civil and political rights	Population	Support for RN Small population bias
Weck-Hannemann (1987): Switzerland	1981–82, cross-sectional	OLS	Aid p.c.	Exports Trade Capitalist dummy	Income p.c. Growth rate Need index	Democracy dummy	Population Lagged aid Aid of other donors	No support for DI, RN or GG

Notes

OLS: ordinary least squares; GLS: generalised least squares; WLS: weighted least squares; 2SLS: two-stage least squares; FDI: foreign direct investment; TNCs: trans-national corporations; HDI: human development index; PQLI: physical quality of life index; ACP: Africa, the Caribbean and the Pacific (countries with a special relationship with Europe under the Lomé conventions); EDA: effective development assistance.

Since the role of GG represents a major focus of this book, the relevant literature and its findings are reviewed in somewhat more detail here. Also, there are fewer studies to review, which makes the task more manageable. Most of the existing literature has focused on the case of US foreign aid allocation, particularly with respect to the role of political and civil rights and personal integrity rights (Cingranelli and Pasquarello 1985; Carleton and Stohl 1987; Poe 1992; Abrams and Lewis 1993; Poe and Sirirangsi 1994; Poe *et al.* 1994; Apodaca and Stohl 1999). These studies differ of course in their results from each other, and sometimes substantially so, due to different research designs. Nevertheless, most of these studies come to the result that more respect for political freedom and, albeit less clearly so, respect for personal integrity rights is rewarded with a higher probability of receiving any US aid as well as with a higher level of aid allocated.

Few studies look at the effect of GG on aid allocation by other donor countries. Svensson (1999) examines various donor countries' aid allocation covering the period from 1970 to 1994. He finds that respect for political and civil rights has a positive impact upon whether a country receives any aid at all from Canada, Japan and the US, but not from Denmark, France, Germany, Italy, Norway, Sweden and the UK. He also finds that political and civil rights lead to the receipt of higher total aid flows from Canada, Denmark, Norway and Sweden, the so-called like-minded countries that traditionally put emphasis on democracy and human rights in their development assistance, and the UK. He finds no effect for the large donors Germany, Japan and the US, for which he suggests that political and strategic goals render rewarding democratic regimes unimportant. Similarly, no effect is found for France and Italy, for which colonial ties play by far the largest role in determining aid allocation. These results are somewhat questionable given that Svensson fails to control for variables of DI. Alesina and Dollar (2000) control for some variables of DI in a study of the period 1970–1994. They come to the conclusion that the fourteen donors they look at differ from each other. They find that political rights have a positive impact on the amount of aid allocated by Australia, Canada, Germany, Japan, the Netherlands, the Scandinavian countries lumped together, the UK and the US, but not by Austria, Belgium, France or Italy. Hence, whilst they confirm Svensson's finding with respect to the like-minded countries, the UK, France and Italy, they come to more positive conclusions about Germany, Japan and the US. Neumayer (2003c) analyses bilateral aid allocation by all twenty-one countries that form the OECD-DAC over the period 1985–1997. In addition to respect for civil and political rights ('democracy'), he also looks at personal integrity rights. He finds that respect for civil and political rights plays a statistically significant role for almost all aid donors on whether a country is deemed eligible for the receipt of aid. However, only the like-minded countries with the exception of Sweden, as well as Germany, Italy, Japan, Luxembourg, Switzerland, the UK and the US also provide more aid to more democratic regimes. Personal integrity rights, on the other hand, are insignificant at best and exert a negative influence on aid eligibility at worst. Only Australia, Denmark, Japan, New Zealand and the UK are estimated to give more aid to countries with a greater respect for these rights. Interestingly, these rights play a role in the aid allocation by few donors only and there is no systematic difference apparent between the like-minded countries and the rest of donor countries as concerns the impact of respect for personal integrity rights on aid allocation. This stands in striking contrast to the self-proclaimed commitment of the like-minded countries with respect to the importance of human rights in their development assistance. A major setback of this study is that GG is only represented by two variables instead of being tested more comprehensively, which is what this book's analysis does.

Neumayer (2003a) addresses regional multilateral development banks and three UN agencies, namely the United Nations Development Programme (UNDP), the United Nations Children's Fund (UNICEF) and the United Nations Regular Programme of Technical Assistance (UNTA). He finds that greater respect for civil and political rights are associated with higher receipts of aid only in the case of the Inter-American Development Bank and in the case of UNICEF and UNTA, but only in some model estimations. These rights also play a statistically significant role at the aggregate multilateral level. This result is confirmed by Neumayer (2003b) in a somewhat different research setting who also finds that civil and political rights matter at the aggregate bilateral level. At that level, improvements in personal integrity rights are also rewarded by higher aid flows, whereas these rights play no role at the aggregate multilateral level.

As concerns the impact of corruption on aid allocation, Alesina and Weder (2000) find no statistical evidence that more aid goes to less corrupt countries in the case of American, British, Canadian, Dutch, Italian, Japanese, German, French, Portuguese, Spanish and Swiss aid. Only for Australia and the Scandinavian donors lumped together is there some evidence that low corruption is rewarded with higher levels of aid. Svensson (2000) also fails to find evidence that countries with less corruption are systematically rewarded with higher levels of combined bilateral and multilateral aid. Similar evidence for the non-importance of corruption levels in the allocation of aid is found by Neumayer (2003a) for the aggregate multilateral aid flows, the regional development banks as well as three UN agencies.

Hout (2002) in his analysis of Dutch aid allocation is one of the few examples to apply a similarly broad definition of GG as is taken in this book. As is to be seen in Chapter 9, his conclusion is that on the whole variables of GG cannot explain well the Dutch aid allocation in the late 1990s and this conforms well with the analysis here.

Population and income biases

Besides explaining the allocation of aid with the help of the three groups of variables (DI, RN and GG), past studies have pointed out certain systematic biases in the allocation of aid with respect to recipient country's income levels and population sizes. For example, already Isenman (1976) and Dowling and Hiemenz (1985) pointed out that less populous countries receive more per capita aid than more populous ones. A wide range of reasons is offered in explanation of this bias:

- In the international arena, due to the importance of the nation state less populous countries can often have an impact that is more than proportional to their population size. The most obvious examples are votes in assemblies such as the UN General Assembly with its 'one country, one vote' system. In some sense, therefore, less populous countries can be more important for donors than their population share would suggest.
- Donors might not want to give an amount of aid to very small countries that looks derisory, thus leading to higher per capita aid for these countries with very small population.
- Donors might perceive decreasing marginal benefits of aid allocation as population size increases and greater aid effectiveness in small countries.
- Very populous recipient countries might have limited capacity to absorb additional amounts of aid.
- Donors might be reluctant to concentrate aid very heavily in the few very populous countries.

Furthermore, Isenman (1976) and Dowling and Hiemenz (1985) also discussed reasons for a middle-income bias, even though the latter did not find evidence for it in their own study. Very poor countries often tend to receive less per capita aid than less poor countries. Only after a certain income threshold has been reached, the exact location of which differs from donor to donor, do richer countries receive less per capita aid. The reasons for this bias are likely to be manifold again, but the two most important ones are likely to be:

- Very poor countries might be regarded as unimportant and uninteresting in terms of DI.
- Donors might fear that these severely impoverished countries are not able to administer larger aid inflows connected to which might be the perception that aid is relatively more effective in countries with somewhat higher income levels.

As can be seen from the overview in Table 3.1, many studies confirm the bias towards less populous countries, whereas the evidence for a middle-income bias is more mixed.

4 Research design

This chapter provides the methodological ground for the estimations in later chapters. The first major section discusses the econometrics of explaining the pattern of aid giving in the context of panel data. The following section explores what should be the dependent variable in the regressions – a question, which has an answer that is less straightforward than one might think. Then follows a presentation of the explanatory or independent variables used, grouped into RN, DI and GG. The chapter closes with a discussion of some remaining statistical issues and an appendix, which explains how the explanatory variables were constructed and were the data came from.

The estimation techniques

Tobit, Heckman or two-part model?

A statistical analysis of the pattern of aid giving is rendered more complicated by the fact that many donors give a positive amount of aid to some recipient countries and nothing to others. The percentage of countries actually receiving positive amounts of aid among all potential recipient countries varies from donor to donor and over time. The big donors tend to give some amount of aid to a great many countries, whereas smaller donors tend to concentrate their aid on a few recipients. For example, Denmark provides any amount of aid only to about 31 per cent of potential recipients in the given sample.

Statistically speaking, what the exclusion of some countries from the receipt of aid by certain donors means is that the dependent variable, aid, is only partly continuous with positive probability mass at the value of zero. Why does this create a problem for standard statistical techniques such as OLS? It is because OLS depends on the assumption that the expected value of the dependent variable (conditional on the explanatory variables) is linear in the explanatory variables, which is violated by the fact that the independent variable has positive probability mass at value zero (Wooldridge 2002: 518). As a consequence, simply applying OLS estimation results in negative predicted values of the independent variable for some values of the explanatory variables, which is clearly undesirable given that the dependent variable is strictly non-negative. If the share of zero values is very small, then OLS estimations are not too misleading, but if it is big, then the problem can no longer be ignored and one has to deal with the fact that the dependent variable has positive probability mass at value zero directly.

What to do then? There are many models in the econometric literature to deal with this type of situation (see Amemiya (1985, chapter 10) for an overview). The three most prominent ones are discussed here. Nomenclature varies, but the first one is often called the (standard) Tobit or type I Tobit model. The second one is called the Heckman sample selection, Heckit or type II Tobit model. The third one is called the two-part model. In the discussion of the three models the formal exposition and technical jargon have been kept to a minimum, but it cannot entirely be avoided.

Let us start with the type I Tobit model. It has its name due to Tobin's (1958) analysis of household expenditures on durable goods, where the dependent variable, similarly to the aid variable, is partly continuous with positive probability mass at value zero since not all households spend some positive amount of their income on such goods. Tobin suggested that in maximising their utility, some households would actually like to spend negative amounts of money on durable goods in order to spend more money on other goods. Of course, that is impossible so that these consumers choose the best available alternative, which is to spend zero on durable goods. In other words, all negative values of the variable 'desired household expenditures on durable consumer goods' are non-observable and, instead, will be recorded at a value of zero. This is why the type I Tobit model is sometimes also called a censored regression model as all negative values are censored to be zero. Formally, the model can be described as follows:

$$
\begin{aligned}
y_i^* &= \alpha + x_i'\beta + u_i \quad i = 1, 2, \ldots, N \\
y_i &= y_i^* \qquad\qquad \text{if } y_i^* > 0 \\
y_i &= 0 \qquad\qquad\ \text{if } y_i^* \leq 0,
\end{aligned}
\tag{1}
$$

where the '*' signals that in principle the respective variables are not observable. The y^* are desired expenditures and y are actual expenditures, α is a constant, x' contains the explanatory variables, β is the corresponding vector of coefficients to be estimated and u_i is the error term, of which it is normally assumed that its expected value is zero and it is not correlated with any of the explanatory variables. Tobin (1958) then went on and derived an estimator for this model. The mathematics is not presented here – the interested reader is referred to Tobin (1958), Amemiya (1985), Verbeek (2000) or Wooldridge (2002). Instead, we will explain in plain words why usage of the type I Tobit model might be inappropriate for the purposes here. To start with, on a conceptual level, it would be rather strange to argue that donors have negative desired levels of aid allocation for some countries. They do not give aid to these countries because they do not want to give them any aid. But one would be hard pressed to argue that, actually, what they want is to give negative amounts of aid and, since it is impossible to extract money from them, they settle for zero. Hence, conceptually the problem at hand does not fit very well the context the type I Tobit model was originally developed for.[1] Of course, one might argue that perhaps this conceptual inconsistency does not matter so much, as long as the model still fulfils its purpose in providing us with accurate answers to the research questions.

What then are the research questions? To recapitulate, in accordance with much of the existing literature, there are two general inquiries. First, given that for the many donors some countries do not receive any aid at all, we seek to explain what determines whether a country is deemed eligible for the receipt of aid. Second, for the sub-sample of countries that receive positive amounts of aid, we seek to explain what determines how much aid a country is given.

How does the type I Tobit model fare in this respect? It can provide answers to both questions, but it does so in a rather restrictive way. First, it assumes that the same variables that determine aid eligibility also determine the amount of aid given. This is possibly a plausible assumption and later chapters will indeed use the same set of variables for explaining both aspects of the research question. But it need not hold true and if the same set of variables are employed for both kinds of estimations, then this should be the consequence of choice, not the consequence of the restrictive character of the model estimator. Second, and more importantly, the type I Tobit model also imposes the constraint that the variables determine aid eligibility and the amount of aid given with the same sign, that is, either positively or negatively. In other words, the model excludes the possibility that higher values of an independent variable makes it more likely that a country is deemed eligible for aid receipt, but also leads to lower amounts of aid actually received once a country has been deemed eligible. Again, this could possibly be a plausible assumption, but this time it is definitely something that should be tested rather than simply assumed. Indeed, part of the research interest lies in finding out whether there are differences in the determinants of aid eligibility and the determinants of the amount of aid allocated. This renders the type I Tobit model uninteresting and inappropriate for our purposes.

The type II Tobit or sample selection model, first developed by Heckman (1979), does not share either restriction, which renders it immediately appealing. As it can be seen further below, it has its own problems, however. Before coming to this, let us understand what the rationale behind this model is. It allows estimation of different determinants of the two stages, namely the aid eligibility stage and the stage where the amount of aid allocated to previously chosen countries is decided. There are hence now two separate equations to be estimated, which are however estimated simultaneously. The first one is:

$$y_i^* = \alpha + x_{1i}'\beta_1 + u_{1i} \quad i = 1, 2, ..., N \tag{2a}$$

The second one is:

$$\begin{aligned} z_i^* &= \alpha + x_{2i}'\beta_2 + u_{2i} \quad i = 1, 2, ..., N \\ y_i &= y_i^* \quad z_i = 1 \qquad \text{if } z_i^* > 0 \\ y_i &= 0 \quad z_i = 0 \qquad \text{otherwise} \end{aligned} \tag{2b}$$

The z_i^* is a binary decision variable on whether or not a country is deemed eligible for the receipt of aid and z_i is its observed counterpart. The y_i are actual levels of aid allocated to eligible countries and y_i^* are potential aid allocations. The latter is of no further interest in this context and is difficult to interpret as it includes the amount of aid that would be allocated to ineligible countries.

Note that the type I Tobit model is a special case of the more general type II Tobit model in that the former follows from the latter in setting $x_{1i}'\beta_1 = x_{2i}'\beta_2$ and $u_{1i} = u_{2i}$. Of course, as argued above, there is no reason to simply assume this to be the case in the context of aid allocation. Hence, naturally the preference for the more general model, type II Tobit. Also note that for this model the errors from both estimations could be correlated such that $\text{COV}(u_{1i}, u_{2i}) \neq 0$. Heckman (1979) showed that if this covariance is not equal to zero, then in the current context simply applying OLS to estimate equation (2a) leads to biased estimation results. He also developed an estimator that corrects for the bias introduced by the correlation of the error terms.

So far, it seems that the sample selection model is ideal for our purposes. Unfortunately, it suffers from its own problems and they are mainly of a statistical nature. The problems will be explained in plain words as far as this is possible, but readers might wish to consult the technical expositions contained in Verbeek (2000) or Wooldridge (2002) for more concise treatments. To start with, the estimation of this model is much helped by the existence of a variable that strongly affects aid eligibility, but not the amount of aid allocated. Strictly speaking, no such so-called exclusion restriction is necessary for estimation, but in its absence identification of the model depends on the non-linearity of one of the estimated parameters only (the so-called inverse mills ratio). The problem is that this parameter is approximately linear over a wide range of its argument (Puhani 2000: 57). One consequence of the absence of an exclusion restriction is that standard errors are often inflated and estimates of equation (2a) are unreliable due to collinearity problems (Vella 1998). Leung and Yu (1996) demonstrate that this represents less of a problem than many others, such as Manning *et al.* (1987) have argued before, but most econometricians would still regard estimation results with great suspicion if no exclusion restriction is present (Breen 1996; Verbeek 2000; Wooldridge 2002).

Why not simply include one then? The problem is that such a restriction is usually difficult to find. What variable would affect only aid eligibility, but not the amount of aid allocated? Most variables one could think of would certainly not fulfil this criterion. For example, the poverty of a country should make it more likely to be eligible for aid, but also more likely to receive a greater amount of aid. Similar reasoning applies to other potential candidates as well. In Neumayer (2003d), I have used the total amount of aid allocated by Arab donors as an exclusion variable. It worked well because the total amount of aid allocated should have no influence on the share of aid allocated to any country and in the specific research design of this article it had a statistically significant, if practically small, positive impact upon the likelihood that a country is deemed eligible for the receipt of Arab aid. Unfortunately, preliminary testing revealed that such a variable does not work equally well for other donors. But if the total amount of aid allocated does not have an impact on aid eligibility, then it is back to square one without an exclusion restriction.

In such a situation, the two-part model, based on Cragg (1971), becomes interesting. It has first been applied on an explanation of aid allocation by Dudley and Montmarquette (1976) and is rather similar to the sample selection model in also estimating separate equations for both stages:[2]

$$y_i | z_i^* > 0 = \alpha + x_{1i}' \beta_1 + u_{1i} \quad i = 1, 2, \dots, N \tag{3a}$$

The second one is:

$$
\begin{aligned}
z_i^* &= \alpha + x_{2i}' \beta_2 + u_{2i} \quad i = 1, 2, \dots, N \\
y_i &= y_i^* \quad z_i = 1 \qquad \text{if } z_i^* > 0 \\
y_i &= 0 \quad z_i = 0 \qquad \text{otherwise} \\
\text{COV}&(u_{1i}, u_{2i}) = 0
\end{aligned}
\tag{3b}
$$

Contrary to the sample selection model, it treats both estimations as independent from each other in assuming that the correlation between the error terms is zero: $\text{COV}(u_{1i}, u_{2i}) = 0$. Also note that it explicitly tests the dependent variable at the level stage conditional on aid eligibility that is for the sub-sample of countries deemed eligible for the receipt of aid only. In the cross-sectional case, equation (3b) is then simply estimated with an appropriate estimator for binary dependent variables such as probit or logit, whereas equation (3a) can be estimated via OLS for the sub-sample of observations with positive values of the dependent variable.

If the correlation between the error terms is truly zero, then the two-part model has many advantages over the sample selection model. No exclusion restriction is necessary and the estimations are also much less vulnerable to model mis-specification. However, if the correlation is not zero, then the second part of the two-part model leads to biased estimates.[3] Monte Carlo experiments have shown, however, that any potential bias of the two-part model is likely to be small in typical situations (Manning *et al.* 1987). The model has been tested for all donors with Heckman's sample selection estimator in order to test whether the correlation of the error terms is zero. In almost all cases, the hypothesis of no correlation could not be rejected at the 5 per cent significance level.[4] As a consequence, the two-part model has been used throughout in the main analysis. Doing so has additional practical advantages in the estimation of panel data, a statistical topic to which let us turn to now. The Heckman sample selection model has been employed in sensitivity analysis, which does not cause dramatic changes to the main results.

Panel data analysis

The data set consists of what is called panel data, since they stem from the same units observed at different periods of time. If the observations at different time periods come from different, but each time random, samples, then one speaks of a pooled data set instead (Wooldridge 2002).

Usage of panel data has many advantages, one being the increase in the precision of estimation due to higher degrees of freedom following from the increase in the number of observations available. It has other advantages as well, which are referred to further below. For now, which estimation technique to be used will be addressed. There are basically four estimators available: OLS, random effects, fixed effects or first differencing. The relative merits of random effects versus fixed effects are looked at first. For simplicity, the focus is on the equation that explains the amount of aid allocated. In a panel data context, this equation could be written as follows:

$$y_{it} = \alpha + x_{it}'\beta + (a_i + u_{it}) \tag{4}$$

Note that contrary to the equations before, a time dimension has also been included to account for the fact that we are dealing with data of both cross-sectional and cross-time dimensions now. Time is indicated by t, countries are indicated by i, y is the amount of aid received, α is a constant, x' contains the explanatory variables, β is the corresponding vector of coefficients to be estimated. The a_i represent *time-invariant* individual country effects. Their inclusion in the model to be tested ensures that unobserved country heterogeneity, that is heterogeneity of countries that is not fully captured by the explanatory variables, is accounted for. Examples are special historic or political relationships not captured by, for example, former colonial experience. The fixed-effects estimator subtracts from the equation to be estimated the over time average of the equation for each country. Because of this so-called within transformation the individual country effects a_i are wiped out and the coefficients are estimated based on the time variation within each cross-sectional unit. The big advantage of the fixed-effects estimator is that any potential correlation of the explanatory variables with the fixed effects is avoided since the fixed effects and therefore their correlation with the explanatory variables are wiped out from the equation to be estimated. Note that without the within transformation correlation of the explanatory variables with the fixed effects would bias the estimations. One disadvantage of using the fixed-effects estimator is that the coefficients of time-invariant variables cannot be estimated. Also, variables with very little variation over time are estimated inefficiently. Technically speaking, an estimator is inefficient if it has a sample distribution with a higher variance than another estimator. What it basically means is that an inefficient estimator estimates the coefficients very imprecisely with unnecessarily large standard errors rendering inference on their statistical significance difficult. The inability of the fixed effects estimator to estimate time-invariant variables and its inefficiency in estimating variables, which vary only little over time, represents a severe disadvantage of this estimator for the purpose here since many of the variables to be tested are either time invariant or vary only very little over time. The same is true for the first-differenced estimator, which is rather similar to the fixed-effects estimator.

The random-effects estimator can estimate time-invariant variables and will estimate all coefficients more efficiently as it uses both the cross-sectional (between) and time-series (within) variation of the data. However, it depends on the assumption that the country effects are not correlated with the explanatory variables so that the individual country effects a_i can be regarded as part of a composite error term $v_{it} = a_i + u_{it}$. This random-effects assumption can be tested with a so-called Hausman test. This tests whether the coefficients estimated by a random-effects estimator systematically differs from the coefficients estimated by a fixed-effects estimator for those variables that can be estimated with the fixed-effects estimator. Only if this test fails to reject the hypothesis that the coefficients do not systematically differ from each other, can it be assumed that the individual country effects can be treated as random effects and can, therefore, be trusted that the estimated coefficients of the random-effects estimator are free from unobserved heterogeneity bias.

How does OLS compare to the random-effects estimator? OLS is inefficient compared to random effects, as it does not optimally exploit the fact that there are observations at various points of time for the *same* set of countries. However, it has one potentially interesting advantage over the random-effects estimator. Contrary to the latter, it does not depend on the assumption that all explanatory variables are strictly exogenous (Wooldridge 2002). Loosely speaking, this implies zero correlation between u_{it} and the explanatory variables in *all* time periods. OLS, on the other hand, only requires that all explanatory variables are predetermined. Loosely speaking, this implies zero *contemporaneous* correlation between u_{it} and the explanatory variables, but u_{it} could be correlated with future values of the explanatory variables. Sometimes it is not easy to decide whether an explanatory variable is strictly exogenous or merely predetermined. In practice, there seem to be few occasions where OLS is preferred over random effects for statistical reasons. As the overview of existing studies in Table 3.1 in the last chapter shows, OLS is a very popular method even for panel data, but this is due to its simplicity and familiarity, not because of superiority on statistical grounds. Therefore, random effects are used throughout the estimations of the amount of aid allocated. In principle, one could also use random effects probit or logit estimators for the equation that determines aid eligibility. However, its estimation in Stata®, the standard econometrics package used throughout this book, relies on quadrature, which performs badly in large panel sizes. Therefore, the standard probit estimator is used.[5]

The Heckman sample selection model is constructed for the cross-sectional case and while the estimator could in principle be adjusted for panel data, there does not exist an easy routine way of estimation, at least not in Stata®. With the two-part model, on the other hand, it is easy to apply panel estimators to (3b) as the two equations (3a) and (3b) are estimated separately. This represents another important advantage of the two-part model over the Heckman sample selection model.

What is aid?

Most people would probably count grants as aid as it is money given away free of charge. But what about money that is lent at an interest rate that is less than the market rate? Should it count as aid as soon as the interest rate is below the market rate or only if it is substantially below the market rate? If the latter, then what is 'substantially' below the market rate? Also, should the loan at less than market rate count fully as aid or only a percentage of it? It can easily be seen that it is not a simple task to determine what should count as aid.

In accordance with the vast majority of the literature, what the OECD defines as ODA is called aid in this book: grants as well as highly concessional loans (i.e. loans with a grant element of at least 25 per cent) that are 'undertaken by the official sector', administered with the 'promotion of the economic development and welfare' of the recipient countries as its main objective (OECD 2002b: 294). Note that the OECD formally distinguishes between ODA, which is assistance going to developing countries, and OA, which mainly consists of assistance going to the Eastern European and Central Asian countries in transition. In this book, instead, both flows are simply called ODA or aid.

ODA or EDA?

World Bank staff members Chang *et al.* (1998) argue that for a whole range of reasons this does not represent the true value of resource transfer from donor to recipient. Two of those reasons are that ODA counts highly concessional loans at their face value instead of at their grant equivalent value and neglects loans with low concessionality even though they have a certain, if low, grant element. They have, therefore, developed a new data set of what they call effective development assistance (EDA) based on the World Bank's Debtor Reporting System that attempts to correct most of the shortcomings of the ODA measure. They also take out ODA in the form of technical assistance as donors often tie such assistance to the condition that goods and services are bought from the donor country.[6] In principle, EDA provides a better measure of aid than ODA. However, EDA data are only available at the aggregate bilateral and multilateral level and even then not for all countries for which OECD provides ODA data. For this reason, the analysis uses ODA data from the OECD throughout the book. The estimations are unlikely to be affected much. First of all, note that for the estimations of the determinants of aid eligibility it is highly unlikely that it matters whether one looks at ODA or EDA since a country that does not receive ODA is also likely not to receive any EDA. Second, even for the actual volumes of aid allocated, Chang *et al.* (1998) note themselves that ODA and EDA data are very highly correlated with each other in spite of differences in their calculation.[7]

Commitments or disbursements?

The next question to decide is whether to look at ODA commitments or disbursements. Commitments are defined by the OECD as 'a firm obligation

expressed in writing', whereas disbursements 'record the actual international transfer of financial resources' (OECD 2002b: 292). Most of the
existing studies analyse disbursements, but some look at commitments.
White and McGillivray (1995: 166) argue that commitments are the more
relevant variable if one wants to analyse the determinants of aid allocation
by donors as commitments are 'the decision variable of the donor' over
which they exert full control, whereas disbursements partly depend on
whether the prospective recipient country actually requests the commitment, which for a number of reasons sometimes is not the case. The commitment data is used wherever these are available and disbursement data
only in the case of Arab multilateral aid. The estimations are unlikely to be
affected much by the choice of commitments over disbursements as the two
are highly correlated for obvious reasons.

Total aid or aid per capita?

The existing literature disagrees on whether total aid should be the dependent variable or aid per capita. The latter elegantly controls for the fact that
countries differ tremendously in their population sizes. If total aid is taken
to be the dependent variable, then at the least population size *must* be one
of the explanatory variables to account for the fact that, all other things
equal, China is likely to receive more aid than, say, Dominica. Which variable to choose should be the result of a careful consideration of the way
donors are likely to allocate aid and should approximate their actual
decision-making behaviour best. In most cases, it seems reasonable to
presume that there is an overall fixed amount of money to be allocated.
Given this overall constraint, McGillivray and Oczkowski (1992: 1314) are
correct in arguing that 'distributing aid in per capita terms in this context is
both a difficult and cumbersome task' as care needs to be taken neither to
overshoot nor undershoot the fixed overall amount of money available. It is
much easier for donors to allocate a share of the total amount of aid available to each recipient country. As McGillivray and Oczkowski (ibid.) point
out, in this process of dividing the cake 'aid decision makers may well be
aware of the corresponding per capita amounts, and may well adjust
absolute amounts on this basis, but this is taken to represent a response to
country size. In this context, per capita aid allocations are viewed as the
outcome of this process rather than the prime consideration'. Therefore, the
amount of aid committed to a recipient country is taken as a share or
percentage of the total amount of aid allocated by the donor to be the
dependent variable. It is believed that this variable approximates best the
way donors undertake their aid allocation decisions.

The dependent variables

Aid commitment data were taken from OECD (2002a). Unfortunately, the OECD does not provide complete data on this variable for all donors. For multilateral Arab aid, therefore (gross) aid disbursement as the dependent variable was taken instead. *Gross* aid disbursements have the advantage over net disbursements that they are non-negative and conceptually closer to aid commitments, which also cannot be negative. The reader should note, however, that the difference between gross and net aid disbursements are relatively small due to the very high grant element of ODA, which for most donors is either 100 per cent or close to it. Only Japan (79 per cent) and Spain (82 per cent) had a grant element of less than 90 per cent in the period 1991–1996 (OECD 2002b).

For Arab countries and multilateral Arab agencies, the OECD only provides aggregate data. Until 1992, the Arab country data comprised the combined total for Algeria, Iraq, Kuwait, Libya, Qatar, Saudi Arabia and the United Arab Emirates (UAE). From 1993 to 1996 the data covered Kuwait, Saudi Arabia and the UAE only, by far the most important donors. No data for the UAE are available for 1997 onwards. The reader should note that whilst these data are the best available, they are also somewhat incomplete because Saudi Arabia keeps secret the geographic allocation of a large part of its aid flows from the Saudi Ministry of Finance (Van den Boogaerde 1991: 27). With respect to the Arab multilateral agencies, the data comprise the combined total for the Arab Bank for Economic Development in Africa, the Arab Fund for Economic and Social Development, the Islamic Development Bank and the OPEC Fund for International Development. Of course, strictly speaking neither the Islamic Development Bank nor the OPEC Fund are exclusively Arab financed institutions, but the Arab countries are by far the major financiers (Porter 1986; Meenai 1989).

As concerns the criterion for aid eligibility a country is called eligible for aid if it gets any positive amount of aid commitment or disbursement. This is in accordance with common usage in the aid allocation literature. Against this, McGillivray and Oczkowski (1992) use a 'significant' aid amount as the cut-off point for aid eligibility. They argue that for many donors, particularly the big ones, aid flows 'tend to be scattered among many countries' in that 'numerous relatively very small and insignificant allocations' are given to many countries, for which they suggest that 'aid decision makers do not fully and seriously consider these allocations' (p. 1312). Whilst there is some truth in McGillivray and Oczkowski's argument about the problem is that the choice of a positive cut-off point is essentially arbitrary. When is an aid allocation so small as not to count? What is known for sure is that a country that does not receive *any* amount of aid at all is definitely regarded as ineligible for the receipt of aid, which is why the common usage of zero as the cut-off point is adhered to.

The explanatory variables

In accordance with the literature on aid allocation variables that cover RN, DI as well as aspects of GG are included. The choice of variables was undertaken with a view towards maximising the sample. In other words, the aim was to have variables that, if at all possible, are available for all countries for which OECD provides aid data. The justification for this is to avoid selection bias, which occurs if data are not randomly, but systematically, missing. For example, very poor, very undemocratic and countries at the verge of collapse of state order often have poor data availability for many variables. Their exclusion would systematically bias the estimations, which is why the maximum sample size possible is aspired to be reached.[8]

There is one potentially important variable not included in the analysis, namely what is called absorptive capacity. This refers to alleged limits of some recipient countries to absorb, that is productively use, further increases of aid inflows. The concept is rather vague as it is far from clear when these limits have been reached and what causes aid inflows to become unproductively used. Berg (1997: 83) suggests that 'high levels of assistance (…) overwhelm local administrations and impact perversely on local ability to manage resources'. She also argues that 'a heavy aid presence is anti-capacity development because it allows local political leaders to postpone hard decisions, induces policy passivity, and distorts the policy environment' (ibid.: 89). Whilst these arguments might be correct, there can be no general rule that an aid to GNI ratio of, for example, 5 per cent suggested by Berg (1997: 91) is the limit of absorptive capacity for all countries. Therefore this variable is omitted as there simply is no good way to measure absorptive capacity. A brief description of the variables used is given here. A more detailed description together with the data sources used is left to the appendix to this chapter.

Recipient need

The single most common, arguably most relevant indicator and frequently only variable of RN included in studies of aid allocation is a country's level of income. Ideally, it represents the power of the average citizen to purchase the goods and services for the benefit of his or her welfare. The lower this power is, the poorer on average a country is and therefore the more in need of aid. In its guidelines on poverty reduction, the OECD-DAC states clearly that aid should be concentrated on the poorest countries (OECD 2001: 60).

Of course, income is an imperfect indicator of RN. Average income levels do not tell us anything about the distribution of income nor is income everything that is relevant for the welfare of people. The deficiencies of per capita income as a comprehensive indicator for the well-being of a country have long since been recognised and lamented (see, e.g. Morawetz 1979; Morris 1979; Hicks and Streeten 1979; Sen 1985; Moon 1991; Moon and Dixon 1992). If low well-being reflects high need for foreign aid, then using only per capita income as a variable does not adequately and comprehensively reflect RN. In spite of this, the existing literature has often only used per capita income, first because it is more readily available than many other potential candidates and second because some do argue that in spite of its problems per capita income remains the single most comprehensive proxy for well-being and therefore for signaling a country's need for aid (see, e.g. Larson and Wilford 1979; Easterly 1999). To test the effect of other aspects of RN on aid allocation the so-called Physical Quality of Life Index (PQLI) is used here in addition to per capita income. It has first been developed by Morris (1979) in a report published for the Overseas Development Council and has been used for example by Maizels and Nissanke (1984) in their early analysis of bilateral and multilateral aid flows and by Tsoutsoplides (1991) in her work on EC aid allocation. The PQLI is an aggregate measure of life expectancy, infant mortality and literacy and is conceptually close to the perhaps better-known Human Development Index (HDI) in its focus on aspects of human rather than merely economic development.[9] However, it has the additional advantage that, contrary to the HDI, income itself is not included as a component so that income per capita and PQLI can be used simultaneously in estimations. The per capita income is taken as a proxy for economic development need and the PQLI as a proxy for human development need.

Of course, one could think of further variables of RN. There are, for example, further variables of economic need, such as the level of indebtedness of a country. However, no further variable is included here for two reasons: First, it is questionable whether further variables of economic need are not simply redundant as the ultimate indicator of economic need is per capita income. Second, and more importantly, any of the further variables of RN included in existing studies of aid allocation suffers from gaps in data availability, which would defeat the aim of maximising the sample of observations.

Donor interest

A whole range of variables that cover different aspects of DI was used. First, where relevant, a variable is used to measure the number of years a recipient country has been a colony of the donor in the last century. Former colonial powers usually have remaining political, economic, cultural and other interests in their former colonies. Where a donor has no former colonies or in the case of multilateral and aggregate aid flows, the relevant variable is the number of years the recipient country has been a former colony of any of the Western countries. This is in order to check for a former colonial experience bias for these aid flows as well. Second, a variable measuring the amount of goods and services exported from the donor to the recipient country as a share of total donor exports is used. This variable functions as a proxy for the commercial or trade interest of donors. Third, to see whether donors give preference to countries, in which they have a military-strategic interest, a variable measuring the share of US military grants to this country is included. The idea behind using this variable is that countries that receive high US military grants can be regarded as allied to Western donors and strategically important countries. Ideally, the inclusion of similar information from other countries would have been desirable, but no sufficient data exist. Fourth, since it is in donors' interest to give aid to 'friendly' and 'close' countries, two variables trying to approximate this interest are employed. As a proxy for converging political viewpoints a political similarity variable that draws from voting behaviour in the UN General Assembly was used. As a proxy for cultural similarity the percentage of Christian people living in a recipient country for Western donors, the percentage of Buddhist people for Japan and the percentage of Muslims for Arab donors was used.

In addition, a number of variables are used that specifically capture aspects of DI by Arab countries: a dummy for Arab countries and a dummy for Sub-Saharan African countries, given the importance that intra-Arab and Arab–African solidarity plays in official statements of Arab donors. Finally, a dummy is included for countries with diplomatic relations to Israel, which might have a negative impact on receiving aid from Arab donors.

Good governance

It is obvious that it is no easy task to measure such a complex entity as GG with some reliability. Nevertheless, various variables are employed that attempt to cover the whole range of aspects of GG in accordance with the broad definition of GG in Chapter 2. Having said this, if donors are truly committed towards strengthening GG in recipient countries, then they should also invest more into developing better quality indicators of governance than perhaps currently exist.

A variable measuring respect for basic human or personal integrity rights as codified in the political terror scales (PTS) is used. Another one measures respect for political rights and civil liberties. The major difference between personal integrity rights and political/civil rights lies in two things: personal integrity rights violations are without doubt non-excusable and are not subject to the relativist challenge.[10] There simply is no justification whatsoever for political imprisonment, torture and murder. Governments that employ or tolerate such activities are guilty of political terrorism (hence the name of the scales). Political/civil rights violations do not carry quite the same status. While such arguments are erroneous in the view of this author and many others,[11] the argument that these rights are contingent on a particular form of Western culture and that a certain amount of political/civil rights violations are somehow 'necessary' for the stability of certain countries and the welfare of their people cannot be as readily dismissed as the argument that political imprisonment, torture and murder are 'necessary' for the same purpose. In this sense, McCann and Gibney (1996: 16) are correct in arguing that the PTS refer to 'policies within the developing world which all theorists and investigators would agree constitute egregious miscarriages of political authority' and represent 'the most serious form of human rights abuses'.

Note that the measures used in this study only capture what is sometimes called first-generation rights, but not economic and social rights, sometimes also called second-generation rights. There are mainly two reasons for this exclusion. First, governments can be better held responsible for violations of first-generation rights than for economic and social rights. Respect for the latter rights can be partly or wholly outside the reach of realistic governmental action. It is difficult to discern whether a low achievement on economic and social rights is a consequence of neglect or malevolent governmental activity or simply the consequence of a country's poverty. Second, and related to this, low achievement of these rights might be reason for the receipt of more rather than less aid. The reason is the overlap with a country's need for foreign aid. Countries with low income per capita and a low score on the PQLI are more in need for foreign aid, but are also less likely to satisfy economic and social rights.

Similarly uncovered from the operational definition of human rights employed in this chapter are cultural rights as well as rights for particular groups – for example, women's rights, rights for gay people and rights of ethnic minorities. The reason for this exclusion is not that I would disregard their importance. It is probably true that, again, governments can be better held responsible for violations of personal integrity and political/civil rights than for these other rights, given that disrespect for these rights is usually an undesirable, but nevertheless integral part of social conventions, norms and behaviour. However, this alone would not represent enough reason to exclude them. Rather, they cannot be included because no comprehensive quantitative index for their measurement is available.

Besides human rights, further variables of GG measure respect for the rule of law, the regulatory burden imposed on the private economy, the perceived extent of corruption as well as the share of government expenditures spent on military purposes. Note that with respect to the latter, ideally a variable that measures 'excessive' military expenditures should have been included, where excessive means expenditures that go beyond what is necessary to fulfil the reasonable security interests of the country. However, it is impossible to establish a threshold for each country beyond which military expenditures become excessive. As an unavoidable shortcut, therefore, it is simply assumed that the lower military expenditures are, the better a country satisfies this aspect of GG.

Note that of all the aspects of governance, 'regulatory burden' on the private economy is probably the most contested and problematic one. It is strongly related to a particular neo-liberal view on economic policy, whereas the other aspects of governance are more consensually accepted across the political spectrum. It is nevertheless included in the analysis since many donors regard low regulatory burden on the private economy as an important aspect of GG.

Remaining statistical issues

Testing for population and income biases

Existing studies testing for population and income biases in aid allocation have mainly used aid per capita as the dependent variable (see Table 3.1 in the preceding chapter). With the dependent variable being the logged share of total aid, testing for population bias is still relatively easy. Note that the estimated coefficient of the logged population variable has an elasticity interpretation. That is, it shows by how many per cent the share of aid received increases if population increases by 1 per cent. If the estimated coefficient is less than one, then there is evidence of a population bias since increases in population are matched with less than proportional increases in the share of aid received. It is not quite as straightforward to test for middle-income bias and there are various ways one could do this. A simple approach is taken that is similar to our test for population bias. It concludes that a donor exhibits a middle-income bias if the estimated coefficient of the logged income variable is smaller than minus one. If it is, this implies that increases in income are matched with less than proportional decreases in the share of aid received, which can be interpreted as a middle-income bias.

Multicollinearity

The reader might wonder whether multicollinearity might pose a problem. What it means is that if there is high correlation amongst the explanatory variables then the estimator sometimes cannot decide well, which variable is responsible for which effect on the dependent variable. This is particularly often the case if there is little variation in the dependent variable. As a consequence, the standard errors are very high and the estimations are usually very sensitive towards the exclusion of some observations as well as to dropping some variables from the model to be tested (Maddala 2000). There are a number of variables for which one might suspect potential problems with multicollinearity. For example, income and the PQLI are highly correlated as are some of aspects of GG.[12] However, the number of observations and the variation in our dependent variable are usually quite big. In dropping some observations as well as explanatory variables we did not find any evidence that multicollinearity would pose a problem. In addition, variance inflation factors are computed. The individual as well as the mean factor is typically well below 3 and always below 5.5. Whilst not representing a conclusive test (Maddala 2000), this provides some further tentative evidence that there need not be any concern about multicollinearity (Kennedy 1992).

The sample

The sample covers the period 1991–2000 and in principle contains all countries for which OECD provides aid data. The OECD data cover basically all countries in the world minus, obviously, the OECD donors themselves as well as Andorra, Aruba, Bermuda, the Cayman Islands, the Faeroe Islands, Greenland, Iceland, Liechtenstein, Mayotte, Monaco, New Caledonia, the Northern Mariana Islands and San Marino. Unfortunately, a number of countries is lost due to lack of data in the explanatory variables. These include Antigua and Barbuda, Barbados, Belize, Bhutan, Botswana, Brunei, Burkina Faso, Cape Verde, Central African Republic, Comoros, Djibouti, Dominica, Equatorial Guinea, Eritrea, Fiji, Gabon, Grenada, Maldives, Malta, the Marshall Islands, Mauritius, Micronesia, Mongolia, North Korea, Palau, Qatar, Samoa, São Tomé e Principe, the Seychelles, Slovakia, the Solomon Islands, St Kitts and Nevis, St Lucia, St Vincent and the Grenadines and Vanuatu. It can be seen that data are missing mainly for countries with a very small population. There is no reason to be concerned that the remaining sample of countries is unrepresentative as the countries with missing data represent a very mixed group on all the explanatory variables apart from population.

Model specification

All time-varying explanatory variables enter the regressions with a one-year lag to mimic the data situation facing allocators of aid commitments at the time of decision-making. Some studies use a two-year lag instead. There is no correct way of lagging time-varying explanatory variables. Non-reported sensitivity analyses showed that the results remain valid with a two-year lag as well.

The dependent variable was logged to render its distribution less skewed. As concerns explanatory variables, the population, income and exports variables were logged in order to allow an elasticity interpretation of their coefficients. If both the dependent and the explanatory variables are in logged form, then the respective coefficient can be interpreted as stating by how many per cent the dependent variable is increasing or decreasing given a 1 per cent increase in the explanatory variable. An elasticity interpretation makes perfect sense for the population, income and exports variables, for which per cent increases carry substantive meaning. For example, it is clear what is meant by 1 per cent more income. For some variables, a 1 per cent increase does not carry any substantive meaning, however. For example, what does 1 per cent more democracy or respect for the rule of law mean? This is why no log transformation was undertaken for the other variables. Sensitivity analysis showed that the results of our analysis would not be dramatically different if the logged variables were kept in their original unit or if the non-logged variables were in fact logged.

All estimations are undertaken with standard errors that are robust towards arbitrary heteroscedasticity and serial correlation. In addition, standard errors allow for the possibility that observations are clustered, that is, they are assumed to be independent merely across, but not necessarily within countries over time. For completeness, we report the log likelihood of each model, which can be interpreted as a measure for the fit of the model. However, whilst a lower log likelihood in principle suggests better model fit, it has no easy interpretation as the R^2 for linear regression models has and we will not discuss it further in presenting our regression results.

The first stage probit estimations additionally include T-1 year-specific time dummies. Their inclusion lets each time period have its own intercept to allow for aggregate time effects that affect all countries such as changes in the total amount of aid allocated. No such time dummies are needed at the level stage since the dependent variable is the share of aid received by a country in any given year for which aggregate time effects do not matter.

Appendix: description of the way in which the explanatory variables are constructed

In this appendix the sources and the way in which the explanatory variables are constructed are described.

• Income: GDP per capita data in purchasing power parity were generally taken from World Bank (2001). The income data were converted into constant US$ 1997 with the help of the US GDP deflator. Missing income data were taken from estimations undertaken for WHO (2000). For the very few cases, in which this source did not provide a full time series and provided an income estimate for 1997 only (usually small, very poor or war-torn countries), this income level was taken for the whole time series. Whilst this creates a small bias for the estimations, the bias from the alternative possibility, which is deletion of all observations for the country other than 1997, is likely to be greater.

- PQLI: The index has been computed from base data contained in World Bank (2001) according to the formulas provided by Morris (1996). It runs on a 0 (worst) to 100 (scale) and consists of three equally weighted sub-components: literacy, infant mortality and life expectancy at age one. The literacy rate is already on a 0–100 scale. For the infant mortality rate, a mortality of 250 per 1,000 live births is assumed to be the worst performance and no mortality the best performance. The infant mortality rate (IMR) per 1,000 live births is thus converted to a 0–100 scale via the formula $(250 - IMR)/2.5$. For life expectancy at age one (LE1), thirty-eight years is assumed to represent worst performance and 85 years best performance such that it is transformed to a 0–100 scale via the formula $(LE1 - 38)/0.47$.

- Colonial status: This is measured by the number of years a country has been the colony of the donor country in the period 1900–1960. The relevant variable for donors without former colonies and for multilateral and aggregate aid flows is the number of years a country has been the colony of *any* OECD country in the same period. For aid allocation by the EC the variable refers to being a former colony of a member country of the EU. Data are taken from Alesina and Dollar (2000).

- Exports: This is measured as the amount of goods and services in value terms a donor exports to the recipient country as a share of the donor's total exports. Data are taken from OECD (2002c). Only for Arab donors, data are taken from Gleditsch (2001) and refer to the simple average of exports as a share of Kuwait's, Saudi Arabia's and the UAE's total exports. Where appropriate, the relevant variable for multilateral and aggregate aid flows is the weighted average of DAC donors' exports, where the weights are equal to the share of the donor of total DAC aid provided. For aid allocation by the EC a similar variable was created with reference to member countries of the EU.

- US military grants: This is measured as the amount of US military grants a country receives expressed as a share of total US military grants allocated. Data are taken from USAID (2002).

- Political similarity: Signorino and Ritter (1999) have developed a measure of political similarity. This measure conceptualises two political positions as falling within a space defined by all the possible political positions. The measure falls in the interval -1 to 1, where -1 means that two political positions are as far apart in the space as possible (complete dissimilarity) and 1 means that the two political positions are identical (complete similarity). Gartzke *et al.* (1999) use this measure to provide estimates of the similarity of political positions as revealed by the voting behaviour in the UN General Assembly. For the last two years, no data were available and were simply taken to be equal to the data of the latest year available. For Germany, no data were available after 1991. They were substituted with the relevant variable for Austria. The idea is that Austria proxies Germany's political positions well given that it shares the same language and a similar culture with its bigger neighbour. For the Arab countries, the simple average of the values was taken for the major Arab donor countries, namely Kuwait, Saudi Arabia and the UAE. Where appropriate, the relevant variable for multilateral and aggregate aid flows is the weighted average of DAC donors' political similarity, where the weights are equal to the share of the donor of total DAC aid provided. For aid allocation by the EC, a similar variable was created with reference to EU member countries.

- Religious similarity: The percentage of Christian, Buddhist and Muslim people were taken from La Porta *et al.* (2000) and Parker (1997).
- Specific interests of Arab donors: An Arab dummy variable was set to 1 for Bahrain, Djibouti, Egypt, Jordan, Lebanon, Mauritania, Morocco, Oman, Somalia, Sudan, Syria, Tunisia and Yemen. This dummy covers all countries with a majority Arab population, apart from those Arab countries with major oil or gas reserves (Algeria, Iraq, Kuwait, Libya, Qatar, Saudi Arabia and the UAE). An African dummy was set to 1 for all Sub-Saharan African countries except those that are Arab. Lastly, a dummy for relations with Israel was set to 1 if a country had diplomatic relations with Israel, with information taken from Israel Ministry of Foreign Affairs (2000).
- Political freedom or democracy: Respect for political freedom or democracy is measured as the unweighted sum of the political rights and civil liberties index, published by Freedom House (2000). Political rights refer to, for example, the freedom to organise in political parties or groupings, the existence of party competition and an effective opposition as well as the existence and fairness of elections including the possibility to take over power via those elections. Civil liberties refer to, for example, the freedom of the media, the right to open and free discussions, the freedom of assembly, the freedom of religious expression, the protection from political terror and the prevalence of the rule of law (Karatnycky, 1999: 547–9). The two indices are based on surveys among experts

assessing the extent to which a country effectively respects political rights and civil liberties, both measured on a 1 (best) to 7 (worst) scale. A combined freedom index was constructed by adding the two indices and reverting the index, such that it ranges from 2 (worst) to 14 (best). Using Freedom House data over a period of time is not unproblematic since the scale, with which countries are judged, changes slightly over time and it is not designed as a series. Indeed, some cases (e.g. Mexico and Uruguay) rise and fall along the scale in association with global changes in the number of countries that are democratic in years in which these countries exhibited no institutional change. This is particularly problematic in the middle parts of the Freedom House scale. However, Freedom House data are available for many more countries than, for example, the so-called Polity data (Gurr and Jaggers 2000), which do not suffer from this problem, and are therefore used here. Sensitivity analysis showed that our results are not much affected if Polity data are used instead.

- Human rights: Respect for human or personal integrity rights is measured with data from the two Purdue Political Terror Scales (PTS) in accordance with existing aid allocation studies. Even though there is some overlap with the concept of civil liberties from Freedom House, these scales have a much clearer focus on what constitutes arguably the very core of human rights and they are not simply redundant. One of the two PTS is based upon a codification of country information from Amnesty International's annual human rights reports to a scale from 1 (best) to 5 (worst). Analogously, the other scale is based upon information from the US Department of State's Country Reports on Human Rights Practices. Codification is according to rules as follows:

1 Countries ... under a secure rule of law, people are not imprisoned for their views, and torture is rare or exceptional.... Political murders are extraordinarily rare.
2 There is a limited amount of imprisonment for non-violent political activity. However, few are affected, torture and beatings are exceptional .... Political murder is rare.
3 There is extensive political imprisonment, or a recent history of such imprisonment. Execution or other political murders and brutality may be common. Unlimited detention, with or without trial, for political views is accepted ....
4 The practices of Level 3 are expanded to larger numbers. Murders, disappearances, and torture are a common part of life .... In spite of its generality, on this level violence affects primarily those who interest themselves in politics or ideas.

5   The violence of Level 4 has been extended to the whole population .... The leaders of these societies place no limits on the means
or thoroughness with which they pursue personal or ideological
goals.

The simple average of the two scales was used for the present study. If
one index was unavailable for a particular year, the other one available
was taken over for the aggregate index. The average was then reversed
such that the index runs from 1 (worst) to 5 (best). Data are taken from
Gibney (2002). Cingranelli and Richards (1999) provide an alternative
indicator of respect for personal integrity rights to the PTS used in the
main analysis of this book. They claim that their indicator is superior
since their so-called Mokken Scaling Analysis leads to an indicator that
is unidimensional and contains information not only about the level of
respect, but also about the pattern and sequence of respect for particular personal integrity rights. Their indicator was used only in sensitivity analysis since at the time of writing it was still only available for
substantially less countries than the PTS and with some time gaps as
well, even though estimation of this variable for many more countries
and time periods is under way.

- Military expenditures: This is measured as the percentage of central
  government expenditures for military purposes with data taken mainly
  from World Bank (2001). Unfortunately, there are many gaps, which
  were filled with information taken from US Bureau of Arms Control
  (1995, 1998), Encyclopedia Britannica (2001) and using interpolation
  as well as extrapolation for missing years.
- Corruption: Corruption is measured by two variables. First, an index
  for a country's perceived level of corruption was taken from the governance indicators data set created by World Bank staff (Kaufmann *et al.*
  1999a,b). Their so-called graft indicator is defined as the acceptance of
  money for providing extra-legal favours. As corruption is not objec-
  tively measurable, the indicator provides a subjective assessment of the
  perceived level of corruption in a country, which is defined as 'the
  exercise of public power for private gain' (Kaufmann *et al.* 1999a: 8).
  The variable is based on several different sources, partly polls of
  experts, partly surveys of residents and entrepreneurs within a country.
  A linear unobserved components model is used to aggregate these various sources into one aggregate indicator. The advantage of such aggre-
  gation is that the underlying concept is measured with higher reliability
  and data become available for many more countries than would be possible if using one source only. It is normalised such that it ranges from

around −2.5 to 2.5 and has a mean of zero and a standard deviation of one. Higher values signal lower perceived levels of corruption. One disadvantage of this indicator of corruption is that all data underlying the unobserved components model stem from a single, but varying time period around the mid-1990s. This is likely to lead to somewhat biased results since corruption is not a constant, but is evolving over time. However, given that the study is confined to the period of the 1990s, the bias is likely to be small given that corruption is not likely to change very rapidly over such a relatively short period of time.[13] Still, the time-invariance remains a problem and in sensitivity analysis we have therefore substituted this variable with a time-varying variable measuring corruption, which is taken from the International Country Risk Guide (ICRG). Whilst data from this private company, which provides information to international business, are normally prohibitively expensive to get for researchers, data covering the period 1990–1995 were made freely available by King and Zeng (2001) and later data by courtesy of the company. The indicator runs from 0 (worst) to 6 (best). The ICRG website (http://www.icrgonline.com) defines corruption as excessive patronage, nepotism, job reservations, 'favor-for-favors', secret party funding, and suspiciously close ties between politics and business. It is thus somewhat broader in its definition of corruption than the World Bank source. Note, however, that the ICRG variable forms one component of the World Bank variable. If time variation is the major advantage of the ICRG variable, then the fact that the variable is available for much less countries than the World Bank variable is its major disadvantage. This is also the reason why the World Bank variable is the preferred one for the main analysis.

- Rule of law: As with corruption, two variables are employed for this aspect of GG. The first time-invariant one derives from the already mentioned World Bank data set and represents 'respect for law and order, predictability and effectiveness of the judiciary system, enforceability of contracts'. It is roughly comparable to a time-varying variable from the mentioned ICRG data set called 'Law and order', which forms one component of the World Bank variable and is used in sensitivity analysis. The ICRG website defines it as 'strength and impartiality of the legal system together with the extent of popular observance of the law'.
- Regulatory burden: For this aspect of GG only the respective time-invariant indicator from the World Bank dataset is available and represents 'burden on business via quantitative regulations, price controls and other interventions into the economy'.

5 Aggregate aid, Western bilateral and multilateral aid

We start with aggregate aid flows. We then look at aid from the big Western aid donors and from the like-minded countries, before examining the aid allocation by the major multilateral aid agencies. Arab aid is quite different and will be dealt with separately in Chapter 6.

Aggregate aid flows

Here the estimation results for aggregate aid flows are reported: total aid, bilateral aid from DAC-countries and multilateral aid. Note that for these three categories of aid it does not make sense to distinguish two stages of the aid allocation process as almost all countries receive some positive, if sometimes small, amount of aid. Therefore, results reported here are for the level stage only.

Column I of Table 5.1 starts with total aid flows. More populous and poorer countries receive more aid. The quality of life does not matter in terms of RN once income is controlled for. Countries which import a higher share of general goods and services from Western donors as well as those with a greater share of US military grants receive more aid. Interestingly, however, neither colonial experience, nor religious or political similarity test significantly. As concerns GG, only respect for human rights and low regulatory burden are positively associated with aggregate total aid flows.

How do the results change if the aggregate total aid flows are broken down into aggregate bilateral and aggregate multilateral flows? Column II of Table 5.1 presents results for the latter. There is no difference to total aid flows in terms of statistical significance and signs of coefficients. Column III of Table 5.1 addresses bilateral aid flows from DAC countries. Again, the results are very similar to total aid flows with the exception of the GG variables. Low regulatory burden remains significant at the bilateral level, but respect for human rights becomes insignificant, whereas democracy assumes significance. Contrary to expectation, greater respect for the rule

Table 5.1 Aggregate aid flows (level stage)

	I Total aid	II Multilateral aid	III DAC aid
ln (population)	0.296	0.291	0.343
	(3.66)***	(3.32)***	(3.73)***
ln (GDP per capita)	−0.862	−1.144	−0.802
	(4.97)***	(6.28)***	(3.98)***
PQLI	−0.002	−0.009	−0.001
	(0.22)	(1.27)	(0.13)
Share US military grants	0.019	0.026	0.019
	(5.76)***	(2.62)***	(5.26)***
Former Western colony	−0.001	−0.002	0.000
	(0.28)	(0.61)	(0.03)
Political similarity	−0.297	0.225	−0.194
	(0.93)	(0.52)	(0.63)
ln (exports)	0.194	0.136	0.245
	(2.68)***	(1.89)*	(3.01)***
% Christian	−0.004	−0.003	−0.001
	(1.23)	(0.99)	(0.37)
Democracy	0.026	0.031	0.036
	(1.55)	(1.17)	(2.12)**
Human rights	0.068	0.138	0.039
	(1.80)*	(2.75)***	(0.87)
Military expenditures	−0.004	−0.004	−0.003
	(1.20)	(1.04)	(0.88)
Low corruption	−0.016	−0.061	0.041
	(0.07)	(0.26)	(0.17)
Rule of law	−0.303	−0.141	−0.461
	(1.31)	(0.66)	(1.74)*
Low regulatory burden	0.512	0.404	0.495
	(3.03)***	(2.52)**	(2.51)**
Observations	1,141	1,125	1,140
Number of countries	121	121	121
Hausman-test chi^2	13.35	72.65	13.59
Hausman-test *p*-value	0.1474	0.0000	0.1375
Log likelihood	−1,084.8	−1,599.5	−1,159.0

Notes
Dependent variable is ln (share of aid). Coefficients of constant not reported. Absolute
z-statistics in parentheses.
  * Significant at 10%.
 ** Significant at 5%.
*** Significant at 1%.

of law is marginally significant with a negative coefficient. The Hausman
test rejects the random effects assumption only in the case of multilateral
aid. Closer inspection beyond what is reported in Table 5.1 shows that this
is mainly due to the difference in the coefficients of the population variable

between the random and fixed effects estimation. This makes sense as the variation in this variable across time is very small, whereas it varies considerably across countries. It also suggests that the bias in the other coefficients is likely to be very small.

A striking result of the analysis of aggregate aid flows is the insignificance of the colonial experience variable. It will be seen in the next sections whether this result holds true at the level of individual aid flows as well or whether donor countries differ from each other in this respect. Also interesting are the results on the variables of GG. In all three types of aggregate aid flows, low regulatory burden exerts a consistently positive influence on aid allocation. Greater respect for human rights is associated with an increase in aid at the aggregate multilateral and total level, whereas democratic countries receive more aid only at the aggregate bilateral level. Whilst high performance on these aspects of GG is rewarded, none of the other aspects are. Again, it remains to be seen whether there is more evidence for an impact of GG upon aid allocation once the aggregated aid flows are disaggregated into individual donors, which is what will be done now.

The big bilateral donors: Britain, Germany, France, Italy, Japan and the US

Aid eligiblity stage

Table 5.2 provides information on the results of the gate-keeping stage estimations for Italy, the UK and the US. No such estimations were undertaken for either France, Germany or Japan as all three donors give some positive, if often small, amount of aid to almost all countries. Population size plays a positive role in the aid eligibility decisions in the case of the UK, but not of Italy or the US. As expected, all three donors are more likely to select poorer countries, but the quality of life plays no role once income is controlled for. As concerns DI, the UK selects its former colonies with greater probability and in the case of Italian and US aid allocation all former colonies are eligible for aid in all years. None of the other variables assume statistical significance. Turning towards aspects of GG, democratic countries are more likely to be eligible for aid only in the case of the US, countries with low corruption in the case of the UK and countries with low military expenditures in the case of Italy. The US surprisingly selects countries with greater respect for the rule of law with lower probability. A low regulatory burden renders countries more likely to be eligible for aid in the case of the UK and the US, but not Italy. None of the other variables of GG play any role.

Table 5.2 Big Western aid donors (eligibility stage)

	I US	II UK	III Italy
ln (population)	−0.003	0.033	0.051
	(0.21)	(3.77)***	(1.62)
ln (GDP per capita)	−0.122	−0.080	−0.159
	(4.13)***	(4.28)***	(3.11)***
PQLI	−0.001	0.001	0.001
	(0.78)	(1.23)	(0.30)
Share US military grants	0.002	−0.001	−0.003
	(0.89)	(0.48)	(0.57)
Former own colony	'100% success'	0.001 (1.98)**	'100% success'
Political similarity	0.090	0.030	−0.210
	(1.48)	(0.94)	(1.46)
ln (exports)	0.006	−0.004	0.028
	(0.66)	(0.63)	(1.35)
% Christian	0.000	0.000	0.001
	(0.36)	(0.93)	(1.07)
Democracy	0.010	−0.002	0.000
	(2.09)**	(0.73)	(0.02)
Human rights	0.007	0.000	−0.015
	(0.59)	(0.01)	(0.66)
Military expenditures	0.000	−0.001	−0.002
	(0.30)	(1.14)	(1.80)*
Low corruption	0.034	0.051	0.025
	(1.11)	(2.43)**	(0.39)
Rule of law	−0.097	−0.021	−0.004
	(3.02)***	(0.87)	(0.05)
Low regulatory burden	0.080	0.038	0.049
	(3.30)***	(2.24)**	(1.04)
Observations	1,146	1,156	1,138
Number of countries	121	121	121
Log likelihood	−284	−264	−459

Notes
Dependent variable is aid eligibility dummy. '100% success' means that all former colonies are eligible for aid in all time periods. Coefficients of constant and year-specific time dummies not reported. Absolute z-statistics in parentheses.
  * Significant at 10%.
 ** Significant at 5%.
*** Significant at 1%.

Level stage

Let us turn to the level stage and see whether GG plays a greater role there. Column I of Table 5.3 presents estimation results for Japan. More populous and poorer countries receive more Japanese aid as do those with lower quality of life. The major importers of Japanese goods and services receive more aid as well as countries with a strong Buddhist population and those with a higher share of US military grants. Colonial experience does not play any role. The same is true for political similarity. As concerns

Table 5.3 Big Western aid donors (level stage)

	I Japan	II US	III Germany	IV France	V UK	VI Italy
ln (population)	0.523	−0.001	0.508	0.530	0.622	0.281
	(4.04)***	(0.01)	(4.27)***	(5.67)***	(6.18)***	(2.15)**
ln (GDP per capita)	−0.504	−0.501	−0.845	−0.217	−0.895	−0.790
	(2.34)**	(1.80)*	(3.62)***	(1.19)	(3.28)***	(3.60)***
PQLI	−0.017	−0.007	0.002	−0.008	−0.001	−0.011
	(1.99)**	(0.64)	(0.24)	(1.08)	(0.10)	(1.09)
Share US military grants	0.026	0.025	0.003	0.019	0.022	−0.010
	(4.18)***	(2.19)**	(0.39)	(1.94)*	(1.69)*	(0.50)
Former own colony	−0.147	0.035	0.040	0.053	0.033	0.037
	(1.12)	(4.52)***	(1.06)	(12.05)***	(6.50)***	(4.66)***
Political similarity	0.113	0.085	−0.149	0.286	−0.231	−0.395
	(0.22)	(0.23)	(0.47)	(1.00)	(0.79)	(0.68)
ln (exports)	0.356	0.143	0.226	0.196	0.096	0.082
	(4.09)***	(1.61)	(2.48)**	(3.79)***	(1.13)	(0.98)
% Christian	0.034	−0.007	0.002	0.007	0.006	0.008
	(4.68)***	(1.27)	(0.41)	(1.74)*	(1.37)	(1.70)*
Democracy	0.073	0.082	0.037	0.027	0.025	0.017
	(2.26)**	(3.23)***	(2.06)**	(1.30)	(0.96)	(0.43)
Human rights	0.278	−0.030	0.045	0.026	0.069	−0.157
	(3.89)***	(0.42)	(0.87)	(0.51)	(1.01)	(1.77)*
Military expenditures	−0.003	0.006	−0.012	−0.004	0.000	−0.008
	(0.37)	(0.87)	(2.64)***	(1.08)	(0.03)	(0.89)
Low corruption	−0.897	−0.194	−0.006	0.342	0.048	−0.197
	(2.99)***	(0.51)	(0.02)	(1.50)	(0.15)	(0.65)
Rule of law	0.077	−0.352	−0.059	−0.200	−0.012	0.412
	(0.26)	(1.09)	(0.18)	(0.64)	(0.03)	(1.18)
Low regulatory burden	1.119	0.355	0.266	0.159	0.211	0.438
	(5.10)***	(1.14)	(1.05)	(0.80)	(0.80)	(2.00)**
Observations	1,109	966	1,129	1,125	1,027	923
Number of countries	119	112	120	121	118	112
Hausman-test chi^2	5.38	2.19	−40.37	8.56	54.33	45.51
Hausman-test *p*-value	0.7996	0.9881	n.a.	0.4792	0.0000	0.0000
Log likelihood	−1,768	−1,495	−1,401	−1,437	−1,447	−1,734

Notes
Dependent variable is ln (share of aid). Coefficients of constant not reported. Absolute *z*-statistics in parentheses.
n.a. Not applicable.
   * Significant at 10%.
  ** Significant at 5%.
*** Significant at 1%.

aspects of GG, more democratic countries receive more aid. The same is true for countries with high respect for human rights and low regulatory burden. However, more Japanese aid seems to go to countries with greater corruption.

Column II of Table 5.3 looks at the US. More populous countries do not receive more aid, which is as clear an indication of a bias against more populous countries as is possible. Poorer countries receive more aid, but a recipient country's quality of life has no impact once income is controlled for. More aid goes to former colonies of the US as well as those receiving a higher share of US military grants. None of the other DI variables play any role. As concerns aspects of GG, more democratic countries receive more aid. None of the other variables is statistically significant.

Estimation results for German aid allocation can be found in column III of this table. Poorer and more populous countries receive more aid. The quality of life plays no role as a variable of RN. Former German colonies do not receive more aid. More aid only goes to countries, which are major importers of German goods and services. None of the other DI variables is significant. More democratic countries are again estimated to receive more aid as was the case for the US. The same is true for countries with low military expenditures. None of the other aspects of GG seem to play any role. Note that for negative chi^2 values of the Hausman test as is the case with Germany, no probability level for the rejection of the tested hypothesis (the p-value) can be computed, but negative chi^2 values provide strong evidence that the random effects assumption cannot be rejected (Stata 2001).

French aid allocation is the subject of column IV of Table 5.3. More populous countries receive more aid, but neither poorer countries nor those with low quality of life receive more aid. Of all the major donors, France's aid allocation is therefore least sensitive to the RN. Military-strategic, export and colonial interests all impact upon French aid allocation according to expectation. Predominantly Christian countries also receive more aid. None of the aspects of GG play any role for French aid allocation.

Column V of Table 5.3 presents estimation results for the UK. As before, more populous and poorer countries receive more aid. The UK gives clearly more aid to its former colonies and also to countries receiving a higher share of US military grants. None of the other DI variables matter. GG does not play any role. Finally, Italian aid allocation is addressed in the remaining column of this table. As usual, more populous and poorer countries receive more aid. Former colonial experience and religious similarity are the only DI variables that matter. Italy gives more aid to countries with low regulatory burden, but less aid to countries with high respect for human rights. None of the other aspects of GG play any role. Hausman tests reject the random effects assumption for both British and Italian aid allocation. As with aggregate multilateral aid flows, closer inspection shows that this is mainly due to the large difference in the population coefficient between random and fixed effects estimation.

The like-minded countries: Canada, Denmark, the Netherlands, Norway and Sweden

At the aggregate level as well as in the case of the big bilateral donors it has been seen that GG plays a rather limited role only. The like-minded countries (Canada, Denmark, the Netherlands, Norway and Sweden) have a reputation of being staunch defenders of GG. In particular, the promotion of democracy and human rights supposedly plays an important role in their foreign policy and aid giving. Do aspects of GG play a more prominent role in the aid allocation by these countries?

Aid eligibility stage

Table 5.4 provides information for the aid eligibility stage. All like-minded donors are more likely to select more populous countries. Given that they are all relatively small donors, this is probably the consequence of a desire to concentrate limited aid flows. All donors give preference to poorer countries as would be expected given the traditionally strong focus on poverty allevi-ation of these donors. However, the quality of life does not play a role. The only exception is Sweden, which selects countries with a high physical qual-ity of life index with higher rather than lower probability, however. In line with expectation is the result that DI plays only a limited role. Norway selects countries with a higher share of US military grants with greater prob-ability, Canada the major importers of its goods and services. Only religious similarity plays some more prominent role, with Canada, the Netherlands and Norway selecting predominantly Christian countries with greater prob-ability. As concerns aspects of GG, only the Netherlands gives preference to democratic countries. Only Denmark selects countries with a high respect for human rights and low military expenditures with greater probability. If anything, Norway is less likely to select countries with high respect for human rights. Countries with low regulatory burden are more likely to be eligible to receive Canadian and Danish aid. Canada also gives preference to countries with low corruption at this stage. Strikingly, neither Norway nor Sweden select countries with greater likelihood that perform well on at least one aspect of GG.

Level stage

At the level stage, all like-minded donors give more aid to more populous countries (see Table 5.5). With the exception of Denmark, all give more aid

Table 5.4 The like-minded donors (eligibility stage)

	I Canada	II Denmark	III The Netherlands	IV Norway	V Sweden
ln (population)	0.022	0.094	0.071	0.086	0.085
	(1.71)*	(3.24)***	(3.46)***	(2.43)**	(2.25)**
ln (GDP per	−0.120	−0.305	−0.204	−0.351	−0.396
capita)	(5.04)***	(4.92)***	(4.72)***	(5.92)***	(4.39)***
PQLI	−0.000	−0.001	0.000	0.002	0.008
	(0.54)	(0.36)	(0.19)	(1.01)	(2.04)*
Share US military	−0.002	0.005	0.002	0.012	0.003
grants	(1.35)	(0.72)	(0.77)	(1.90)*	(0.27)
Former own or	0.000	−0.002	0.002	−0.001	0.000
Western colony	(0.13)	(1.52)	(0.61)	(0.72)	(0.07)
Political similarity	0.071	−0.338	0.011	−0.155	−0.351
	(1.16)	(1.55)	(0.13)	(0.78)	(1.43)
ln (exports)	0.013	0.011	−0.014	0.003	0.031
	(1.77)*	(0.40)	(0.78)	(0.17)	(1.11)
% Christian	0.001	−0.000	0.001	0.002	0.002
	(2.44)**	(0.13)	(1.91)*	(2.03)**	(1.30)
Democracy	−0.004	0.014	0.019	0.004	0.017
	(0.81)	(1.04)	(2.98)***	(0.30)	(1.20)
Human rights	−0.004	0.070	−0.011	−0.053	0.019
	(0.35)	(2.21)**	(0.60)	(1.76)*	(0.45)
Military	−0.000	−0.004	0.000	−0.002	−0.002
expenditures	(0.42)	(1.68)*	(0.09)	(0.80)	(0.75)
Low corruption	0.078	0.103	0.052	0.059	0.127
	(2.75)***	(1.46)	(1.20)	(0.84)	(1.29)
Rule of law	−0.042	−0.075	0.031	0.033	0.035
	(1.23)	(0.86)	(0.60)	(0.40)	(0.30)
Low regulatory	0.051	0.181	−0.020	0.029	−0.027
burden	(2.27)**	(2.38)**	(0.50)	(0.48)	(0.35)
Observations	1,156	1,156	1,155	1,156	1,156
Number of countries	121	121	121	121	121
Log likelihood	−293	−579	−384	−411	−526

Notes
Dependent variable is aid eligibility dummy. Coefficients of constant and year-specific time dummies not reported. Absolute z-statistics in parentheses.
   * Significant at 10%.
  ** Significant at 5%.
*** Significant at 1%.

to poorer countries as well and none take the quality of life into account once income is controlled for. As concerns the other variables, starting with Canada in the first column of Table 5.5, major importers of Canadian goods and services and those receiving a higher share of US military grants are estimated to receive more aid. Neither former colonial experience by

Table 5.5 The like-minded donors (level stage)

	I Canada	II Denmark	III The Netherlands	IV Norway	V Sweden
ln (population)	0.528	0.252	0.533	0.333	0.453
	(5.06)***	(1.80)*	(5.06)***	(2.26)**	(3.31)***
ln (GDP per capita)	−0.707	−0.429	−1.008	−0.911	−1.248
	(3.42)***	(1.20)	(3.76)***	(3.57)***	(2.66)***
PQLI	−0.008	0.020	0.001	0.000	0.019
	(0.88)	(1.56)	(0.13)	(0.02)	(0.79)
Share US military grants	0.022	0.023	0.011	0.018	0.002
	(1.75)*	(3.64)***	(0.93)	(2.55)**	(0.17)
Former own or Western colony	0.005	0.011	0.055	−0.001	−0.009
	(1.04)	(1.53)	(2.14)**	(0.10)	(1.19)
Political similarity	0.486	2.491	0.079	0.917	−0.358
	(0.83)	(1.91)*	(0.17)	(1.29)	(0.40)
ln (exports)	0.139	0.103	−0.204	0.068	−0.079
	(2.15)**	(0.92)	(2.79)***	(1.05)	(0.80)
% Christian	0.003	0.001	−0.001	0.009	0.012
	(0.81)	(0.17)	(0.19)	(1.63)	(2.28)**
Democracy	0.024	0.045	0.079	−0.026	−0.031
	(0.96)	(0.92)	(2.08)**	(0.73)	(0.83)
Human rights	−0.112	−0.068	−0.051	0.007	0.138
	(1.53)	(0.49)	(0.59)	(0.10)	(1.15)
Military expenditures	−0.009	0.003	0.012	−0.000	0.004
	(1.66)*	(0.40)	(1.83)*	(0.01)	(0.45)
Low corruption	0.383	−0.463	0.468	0.521	1.388
	(1.41)	(1.08)	(1.31)	(1.26)	(2.95)***
Rule of law	−0.439	0.592	−0.543	0.004	−0.006
	(1.60)	(1.15)	(1.40)	(0.01)	(0.01)
Low regulatory burden	0.559	−0.315	0.546	−0.066	−0.369
	(2.55)**	(0.98)	(1.69)*	(0.22)	(1.05)
Observations	988	422	922	795	552
Number of countries	115	77	113	110	109
Hausman-test chi^2	−2,238.9	−178.2	8.20	12.47	12.07
Hausman-test *p*-value	n.a.	n.a.	0.5141	0.1882	0.2092
Log likelihood	−1,581	−782	−1,661	−1,269	−971

Notes
Dependent variable is ln (share of aid). Coefficients of constant not reported. Absolute *z*-statistics in parentheses.
n.a. Not applicable.
  * Significant at 10%.
 ** Significant at 5%.
*** Significant at 1%.

one of the Western countries, nor political similarity or religious similarity matter. More aid goes to countries with low regulatory burden and low military expenditures. Danish aid allocation, for which results can be found in column II of Table 5.5, favours politically similar countries as well as those receiving a greater share of US military aid. None of the other DI variables play a role, neither do any of the variables of GG. Column III of Table 5.5 presents results for Dutch aid allocation. Former Dutch colonies receive more aid. None of the other DI variables test significantly with the expected sign. If anything, major importers of Dutch goods and services receive less rather than more aid. With respect to GG, democracy and low regulatory burden are the only variables positively associated with aid flows. Surprisingly, high military expenditures are positively associated with aid. Results for Norwegian aid allocation are to be found in column IV of Table 5.5. Norway provides more aid to countries receiving a higher share of US military grants. None of the other variables of DI matter. Neither do any of the variables of GG. Sweden gives more aid to religiously similar countries as can be seen from the last column of Table 5.5, but none of the other DI variables play any role. More Swedish aid goes to countries with low corruption, but none of the other aspects of GG matter.

The big multilateral aid donors

The European Community

Besides providing aid bilaterally, member countries of the EU also provide a substantial amount of aid through the EC itself. Indeed, in this study the share of EC aid of total aid is slightly higher than Germany's bilateral share, the single biggest bilateral aid donor within the EC. Germany is also the biggest contributor to EC aid with a share of about 28 per cent, followed by France (20 per cent), the UK (16 per cent) and Italy (13 per cent) (European Community 2001).

The EC aid started out relatively small and almost exclusively concentrated on the former colonies of European donors in the group of ACP countries. Over time, the EC aid programme grew rapidly and became more global in its focus with the share of ACP countries now being substantially below 50 per cent (European Community 2001). Since the EC gives aid to almost all countries, we only address the level stage, for which Table 5.6 provides information. Political similarity is the only DI variable, which impacts upon aid allocation. None of the other DI variables does, not even the former colonial experience variable, which is only marginally insignificant, however. More populous and poorer countries receive more aid as do countries with a low physical quality of life index. As concerns GG, the EC gives more aid to countries with low military expenditures. None of the other aspects of GG matter, even though the democracy variable is only marginally insignificant. The Hausman test rejects the random effects assumption, but as when this happened before, this is mainly due to the difference in the

Table 5.6 The European Community

	Level stage
ln (population)	0.350
	(3.77)***
ln (GDP per capita)	−0.557
	(3.07)***
PQLI	−0.016
	(2.24)**
Share US military grants	−0.016
	(0.62)
Former colony of EU country	0.007
	(1.52)
Political similarity	0.699
	(1.66)*
ln (exports)	0.059
	(0.92)
% Christian	0.004
	(1.34)
Democracy	0.043
	(1.60)
Human rights	0.040
	(0.59)
Military expenditures	−0.022
	(3.00)***
Low corruption	−0.006
	(0.03)
Rule of law	−0.041
	(0.17)
Low regulatory burden	0.109
	(0.59)
Observations	1,038
Number of countries	120
Hausman-test chi^2	60.35
Hausman-test p-value	0.0000
Log likelihood	−1,679

Notes
Dependent variable is ln (share of aid). Coefficient of constant not reported. Absolute z-statistics in parentheses.
  * Significant at 10%.
 ** Significant at 5%.
*** Significant at 1%.

coefficient of the population variable between random and fixed effects estimation.

The UN agencies

Aid flowing through the UN agencies taken together constitutes about 5 per cent of total aid flows in this study. Given the relative autonomy of the UN from direct Western influence (in spite of Western countries being the major funding countries), one might expect that (Western) DI should not play any role for aid flows from UN agencies. Note that almost all countries receive some positive, if small, amount of UN aid, which is why the aid eligibility stage is ignored. Table 5.7 presents results for the level stage. More populous and poorer countries receive more UN aid. By and large, the DI variables are insignificant as would be expected. However, surprisingly more aid seems to go to countries, which are major importers of goods and services from Western countries. With respect to aspects of GG, none of the variables test according to the expectation. If anything, more democratic countries receive less aid from UN agencies.

The International Development Association

The IDA is the World Bank's aid agency, its arm that provides lending at zero interest rate. It is a very important, if perhaps sometimes underrated, multilateral aid provider, which accounts for about 12 per cent of total aid flows in the sample. In some sense, the true aid content is overstated by this figure as all of IDA aid consists of loans, if interest-free, whereas the great majority of aid by Western and other donors consists of grants rather than loans. Recent calls by the Bush administration of the US to transform the World Bank into an agency providing predominantly grants rather than concessional lending would imply changing the nature of IDA development finance from loans to grants and expanding the IDA at the expense of the other arms of the World Bank group. Such a move is fiercely resisted by the Bank as it correctly anticipates that this would also imply that far less overall money will be channelled through the World Bank since the back flow of money from loans is substantially reduced.

The IDA is a rather peculiar aid donor also due to the fact that there are clear and explicit rules laid down with respect to the criteria driving aid eligibility and the amount of aid allocated. To be eligible, countries have to be a member of the World Bank, their GNP per capita must not exceed a fixed threshold (US$885 in 2002), it must be unable to borrow on market terms from the international financial markets due to lack of creditworthiness and it must implement economic and social policies that in the eyes of the Bank promote

Table 5.7 The UN agencies

	Level stage
ln (population)	0.338
	(4.52)***
ln (GDP per capita)	−0.820
	(4.50)***
PQLI	−0.003
	(0.42)
% US military grants	−0.001
	(0.27)
Former Western colony	0.001
	(0.52)
Political similarity	0.433
	(1.02)
ln (exports)	0.184
	(3.12)***
% Christian	0.002
	(0.81)
Democracy	−0.028
	(1.80)*
Human rights	−0.052
	(1.38)
Military expenditures	−0.004
	(0.89)
Low corruption	−0.016
	(0.07)
Rule of law	−0.044
	(0.24)
Low regulatory burden	0.022
	(0.16)
Observations	1,012
Number of countries	120
Hausman-test chi^2	4.07
Hausman-test *p*-value	0.9065
Log likelihood	−850

Notes
Dependent variable is ln (share of aid). Coefficients
of constant not reported. Absolute *z*-statistics in
parentheses.
  * Significant at 10%.
 ** Significant at 5%.
*** Significant at 1%.

growth and poverty reduction (IDA 2002a). A few countries with limited
creditworthiness are allowed to borrow money from the World Bank on normal
terms as well as receive zero-interest loans from the IDA (so-called 'blend
countries').

Table 5.8 The International Development Association

	I Aid eligibility stage	II Level stage
ln (population)	0.096	0.604
	(2.31)**	(6.09)***
ln (GDP per capita)	−0.494	−0.514
	(5.15)***	(2.89)***
PQLI	0.002	0.011
	(0.64)	(1.65)
Share US military grants	0.004	0.009
	(0.50)	(1.55)
Former Western colony	0.000	−0.004
	(0.13)	(1.22)
Political similarity	0.423	−0.817
	(1.64)	(1.12)
ln (exports)	−0.058	−0.154
	(1.58)	(1.53)
% Christian	−0.003	−0.002
	(2.46)**	(0.43)
Democracy	0.021	−0.023
	(1.46)	(1.08)
Human rights	0.087	0.160
	(2.58)***	(2.13)**
Military expenditures	−0.002	−0.007
	(0.61)	(0.81)
Low corruption	−0.031	−0.250
	(0.35)	(0.89)
Rule of law	−0.046	−0.084
	(0.49)	(0.34)
Low regulatory burden	0.193	0.189
	(2.70)***	(0.76)
Observations	1,154	440
Number of countries	121	62
Hausman-test chi^2		3.30
Hausman-test *p*-value		0.9513
Log likelihood	−452	−605.8

Notes
Dependent variable is aid eligibility dummy and ln (share of aid), respectively.
Coefficients of constant and year-specific time dummies not reported. Absolute
z-statistics in parentheses.
   * Significant at 10%.
  ** Significant at 5%.
*** Significant at 1%.

The main factor determining the amount of aid allocated to eligible recipients is the country's performance on IDA's country ranking, which consists of 80 per cent of the so-called Country Policy and Institutional Assessment (CPIA) and 20 per cent of the so-called Portfolio Performance Rating (ARPP). The CPIA ranks IDA eligible countries on a one to six scale according to currently twenty equally weighted criteria featuring aspects of 'economic management', 'structural policies', 'policies for social inclusion/equity' and 'public sector management and institutions' (IDA 2002b). Before 1998, the CPIA did not include factors referring to institutions, but only to policies. The ARPP measures how well past projects have achieved their development objectives in recipient countries according to internal evaluation studies. In addition, more aid should also go to poorer countries. The IDA has even established and published a formula according to which per capita allocation is determined by the performance ranking and per capita income (IDA 2002b). However, the IDA does not follow its formula rigidly. First, some special preference is also given to Sub-Saharan African countries, but it is not indicated how exactly this influences aid allocation (IDA 2002a). Also, extraordinary country conditions such as high indebtedness as well as limited capacity to absorb additional finance imply that the actual allocations differ from the computed allocations (IDA 1997).

Given the importance of the CPIA and ARPP for IDA aid allocation, such a variable should have been included in the empirical testing. However, whilst the World Bank allows its own researchers access to these data it fails to disclose the data to other researchers (personal communication from Satish Mannan from the Bank's Operations Policy and Country Services section). This is not only ethically dubious from a research methodological point of view, but it also means that unfortunately only the other variables of GG are remaining to see how well they can explain IDA's aid allocation.

Column I of Table 5.8 presents results for the aid eligibility stage. More populous and poorer countries are more likely to be selected. As is expected, none of the DI variables matter. Indeed, if anything, predominantly Christian countries are less likely to receive aid from the IDA. Countries with greater respect for human rights as well as countries with low regulatory burden are more likely to receive IDA aid. At the level stage, for which results are reported in the second column of this table, DI variables are insignificant as is expected. More aid goes to more populous and poorer countries. As concerns GG, more aid goes to countries with greater respect for human rights, but none of the other variables are significant. This suggests that the variables of GG do not seem to be highly correlated with IDA's secret CPIA as otherwise these variables should turn out to be significant.

6   The Arab donors

Distinctive features of Arab aid giving

Table 3.1 in Chapter 3 has shown that there exist many studies examining the aid allocation of Western donors. With the exception of Neumayer (2003d), no study seems to exist that quantitatively analyses aid provided by Arab donors. What does exist are rather descriptive studies that provide rich and detailed information, but cannot give an answer to which factors determine with which importance the allocation of Arab aid (see, e.g. Hunter 1984; Imady 1984; Porter 1986; Nonneman 1988; Van den Boogaerde 1991; Raffer and Singer 1996). This lack of a systematic statistical analysis presents an astonishing gap in the relevant literature given that it is often suggested that Arab aid is different from other aid in being heavily influenced by such factors as, amongst others, Arab and Islamic solidarity.

Arab countries have been very generous donors in the past. Neumayer (2003d) estimates that between 1974 and 1994, Arab countries have provided on average about 1.5 per cent of their GNP as net ODA to developing countries. Arab donors were particularly generous in the 1970s and early 1980s, not least helped by enormous financial surplus from oil and natural gas revenue. The slump in oil and natural gas prices in the mid-1980s also saw a drop in Arab aid allocation. In the early 1990s, Arab donors have still been generous, but no longer outstandingly so. The estimate with the aid and GNI data taken from World Bank (2001) suggests that Arab donors have on an average provided about 0.85 per cent of their GNI in the form of aid. Note that this is still well above the average of Western donors (at less than 0.3 per cent) and well above the 0.7 per cent suggested by the UN.[1] These figures even potentially underestimate the generosity of Arab aid giving. This is because the GNI of Arab aid donors mainly derives from the extraction of non-renewable resources and is likely to be inflated. Since such extraction leads to exaggerated income figures given that the partial liquidation of capital (the resource stock) is erroneously counted as true income (Neumayer 1999, 2000), actual GNI is lower and the aid provision to GNI ratio, therefore, higher than the published figures would suggest (see also Raffer and Singer (1996: 124ff.)). Representatives from Arab donors, therefore, rightly argue that 'Arab aid represents a greater sacrifice' than the aid provided by Western countries given that their aid is 'deducted from income which is in reality a cash exchange for a depletable natural resource' (Shihata 1982: 202).

Critics such as Hunter (1984) have argued that the seemingly generous Arab aid is still likely to be lower and perhaps much lower than the economic loss to developing countries in the form of higher prices for oil and natural gas as a consequence of the exercise of market power by the Organisation of Petroleum Exporting Countries (OPEC), of which Arab countries are the main members. Whatever one might think about such an argument, in principle there is nothing that forces Arab countries to share a substantial part of their wealth, which is undoubtedly built on oil and natural gas, with poorer developing countries in the form of aid. Furthermore, with similar reasoning one could question whether Western countries provide any net financial resources at all to developing countries given the enormous flows of money going out of developing countries in order to serve their debt obligations.

The motives for Arab aid giving and allocation have been controversially discussed in the literature. Scholars from Western countries have often been critical, whereas representatives from the Arab world have been more positive in their assessment, insisting that Arab aid is less motivated by DI and more beneficial to developing countries than Western aid. Representative of the Western critical view is, for example, Hunter (1984: 58) who states that 'the aid policies of the Arab members of OPEC have been motivated first and foremost by their security, politico-ideological and economic objectives'. Representative for the competing Arab view is Shihata (1982: 203f.) who stresses the generosity of Arab aid giving, its untied status, supposed 'geographical diversity' and difference to aid from Western donors, which 'usually confine it to countries that are of obvious economic or political interest' to them in order to achieve such 'typical objectives as securing markets for their products or sources of raw materials, preserving former influence, attempting to acquire new influence, or at least ensuring the neutrality of the aid recipient'.

The relevant literature, which has studied Arab aid allocation, albeit not in a systematic statistical sense, suggests a number of factors, which might influence the allocation of aid by Arab countries and Arab agencies. Starting with what one might call Arab solidarity, there is very little doubt that at least in the beginning years of Arab aid allocation, Arab countries were the main beneficiaries of such aid (Van den Boogaerde 1991). Indeed, in the very early years often only Arab countries were eligible for these programmes. For example, only Arab countries were eligible for the receipt of aid from the Kuwait and the Abu Dhabi Fund for Arab Economic Development until 1974. Still today the Arab Fund for Economic and Social Development gives aid exclusively to Arab countries only. Arab countries like to portray this as a living example of active Arab solidarity of the donor countries with their poorer cousins. More critical voices see it as an attempt to buy off a threat by more populous, envious and greedy neighbours in inducing them to believe that friendly relations are more rewarding than hostility would be (Hunter 1984). However, generally speaking, eligibility and the range of recipient countries widened substantially after the very early periods of Arab aid allocation. Already in 1984, Khaldi (1984: 13), claimed that 'Arab aid is geographically balanced out' and is not heavily biased towards Arab countries.

In addition to Arab countries, many observers also suggest that Sub-Saharan African countries might have been favoured due to the pursuit of Afro-Arab unity and the traditionally strong links between these countries and Arab countries (Simmons 1981: 16). Many Arab countries are located in Africa, have shared a history of colonisation with African countries and have generally supported nationalist liberation movements against the colonisation powers. Again, such potential preference is suggested by the existence of such organisations as the Arab Bank for Economic Development in Africa, established in the wake of the commitments made at the Afro-Arab summit meeting in Cairo in March 1977 (Porter 1986: 53f.).

Besides Arab and African solidarity, another potential preference suggested by, for example, Mertz and Mertz (1983) is with respect to Islamic countries. Khaldi (1984: 13) rejects the suggestion that Islamic countries might be favoured by Arab aid in claiming that 'Arab aid does not have any religious character'. However, suggestive of such potential preference might again be the existence of such multilateral agencies as the Islamic Development Bank, which only funds projects in member countries of the Organization of Islamic Conference.[2] A middle position is taken by Porter (1986: 63) who believes that the 'Islamic connection', whilst existent, 'appears to be of relatively small significance among the motivations underlying the Arab aid effort and its distribution'.

Turning towards more directly political factors potentially influencing Arab aid allocation, Mertz and Mertz (1983: 21) claim that 'political interests dictate the distribution of Arab aid' such that aid allocation might be biased towards countries that are similar in their foreign political positions, in particular with respect to issues concerning the Israel–Arab conflict (similarly, Simmons (1981)). However, the claim that political interests heavily influence the distribution of Arab aid is again rejected by

Al-Ani (1984: 42) who states that many of the recipient countries do not have diplomatic relations with OPEC (and therefore Arab) countries.

Finally, Arab like many other aid donors might take the need of potential recipient countries into account in favouring poorer countries. For example, Al-Humaidi (1984: 60) claims that it has been the general policy of the already mentioned Kuwait Fund to favour 'those countries of the developing world which are more in need of assistance than others'. Similarly, Humaidan (1984: 69) claims that the Saudi Fund for Development 'has tried to focus the benefits of its assistance predominantly on the poorest countries, those having very low per capita income'. The website of the OPEC Fund for International Development assures its visitors that whilst all developing countries are in principle eligible for Fund assistance 'the least developed countries (...) are accorded higher priority' (OFID 2002).

Aid eligibility stage

The problem with all these claims about what determines Arab aid allocation is that their validity can only be tested in a multivariate statistical framework, which is exactly what this chapter sets out to do. Note that as mentioned already in Chapter 4, OECD (2002a) provides only aggregate aid data for bilateral and multilateral Arab aid, no individual country or individual multilateral agency data.

Columns I and II of Table 6.1 provide results for aggregate Arab bilateral and multilateral aid eligibility. At both levels, more populous and poorer countries are more likely to receive Arab aid. Donor interest clearly plays a role at both levels. At the bilateral level, countries with a predominantly Muslim population as well as Arab and Sub-Saharan African countries are more likely to be eligible. Different aspects of DI are significant at the multilateral Arab agency level. Neither Sub-Saharan African countries nor countries with a predominantly Muslim population are selected with a higher probability, whereas the absence of diplomatic relations with Israel and political similarity are significant determinants of aid eligibility at the multilateral, but not the bilateral level. For both levels, Arab countries are more likely to be eligible for the receipt of aid, which is to be expected given the special relations among Arab countries. Imports of Arab goods and services play no role at either level. This is not surprising given the very limited range of products Arab countries export.[3]

Perhaps surprisingly, GG plays some role for being eligible for Arab bilateral aid. Countries with low military expenditures are more likely to be selected for bilateral Arab aid. Democratic countries and those with greater respect for human rights and lower regulatory burden are more likely to

Table 6.1 The Arab donors (bilateral and multilateral)

	I Bilateral (eligibility stage)	II Multilateral (eligibility stage)	III Bilateral (level stage)	IV Multilateral (level stage)
In (population)	0.065	0.057	0.156	0.134
	(3.36)***	(1.97)**	(0.83)	(1.56)
In (GDP per capita)	−0.085	−0.301	−0.134	−0.431
	(1.95)*	(4.07)***	(0.28)	(2.31)**
PQLI	0.001	−0.001	0.028	0.001
	(0.66)	(0.28)	(1.05)	(0.14)
Political similarity	0.126	0.228	−0.960	0.220
	(1.21)	(1.78)*	(0.66)	(0.62)
In (exports)	0.007	0.018	0.004	−0.029
	(0.76)	(1.40)	(0.05)	(1.15)
Dummy Sub-Saharan Africa	0.122	0.048	−0.493	−0.375
	(1.82)*	(0.40)	(0.71)	(1.31)
Dummy Arab	0.252	0.211	1.567	1.158
	(2.44)**	(1.99)**	(1.90)*	(3.52)***
Dipl. relations with Israel	−0.050	−0.279	0.725	0.110
	(0.97)	(4.00)**	(1.73)*	(0.71)
% Muslim	0.003	0.002	0.024	0.001
	(3.93)***	(1.49)	(2.58)***	(0.27)
Democracy	−0.001	0.030	−0.023	0.040
	(0.14)	(2.51)**	(0.26)	(1.04)
Human rights	0.014	0.073	−0.003	0.095
	(0.60)	(2.16)**	(0.01)	(1.14)
Military expenditures	−0.007	0.003	−0.047	−0.001
	(3.51)***	(0.97)	(1.97)**	(0.20)
Low corruption	−0.035	−0.177	−0.407	−0.248
	(0.54)	(2.21)**	(0.55)	(0.92)
Rule of law	0.083	0.063	0.047	0.084
	(1.46)	(0.67)	(0.07)	(0.38)
Low regulatory burden	0.067	0.153	0.277	0.200
	(1.54)	(1.94)*	(0.51)	(0.99)
Observations	1,047	1,164	300	543
Number of countries	122	122	81	92
Hausman-test chi^2			12.07	14.57
Hausman-test *p*-value			0.2092	0.1034
Log likelihood	−452	−586	−666	−792

Notes
Dependent variable is aid eligibility dummy and in (share of aid), respectively. Coefficients of constant and year-specific time dummies not reported. Absolute *z*-statistics in parentheses.
  * Significant at 10%.
 ** Significant at 5%.
*** Significant at 1%.

receive aid from multilateral Arab agencies. However, the same is true for countries with a greater extent of corruption.

Level stage

Regression results for the level stage of Arab aid giving are provided in columns III and IV of Table 6.1. Bilateral Arab aid allocation is statistically independent from the population size as well as the poverty of recipient countries. One might think that this is due to bilateral Arab aid mainly following Arab DI. However, quite astonishingly, the DI variables are often insignificant. There is merely some evidence that more aid goes to Arab and countries with a predominantly Muslim population. Surprisingly, the variable diplomatic relations with Israel is marginally significant with a positive sign contrary to expectation. As concerns GG, countries with low military expenditures receive more aid, whereas none of the other aspects matter. Poorer countries receive more multilateral Arab aid as do Arab countries. However, none of the other DI variables nor any of the variables of GG are statistically significant.

In sum, Arab donors screen countries at the eligibility stage according to population size, poverty, a range of aspects of DI as well as some aspects of GG. The latter result is somewhat astonishing, given that Arab donors are by no means known as explicit or vocal advocates of GG and Arab donors themselves do not fare too well in terms of GG themselves. Once countries have passed the aid eligibility stage, few of the variables, which had an impact at this stage, also determine the amount of aid given. In particular, none of the aspects of GG assume statistical significance, with the exception of military expenditures at the bilateral level.

7 Analysis and discussion of results

Population biases

What role does population size play in the allocation of aid? Table 7.1 provides the answer, indicating whether population size is a significant variable at the aid eligibility stage. It can be seen that the vast majority of donors, particularly the smaller ones, select more populous countries with greater probability. The reason is probably a desire of donors to concentrate their limited funds. In Chapter 3 we have also noted, however, that there is commonly a bias against more populous countries in that population size increases are not matched by proportional increases in the receipt of aid at the level stage. To address this issue Table 7.1 also provides a best estimate of the elasticity of the population variable together with a 90 per cent confidence interval. Due to the impact of randomness on statistical analysis, the estimated coefficients are merely a best estimate, but they are not certainties. Loosely speaking, the confidence interval gives a lower and upper bound and 90 per cent confidence that the true value lies within this interval. On this basis, it is almost certain that all donors have a population bias. This can be discerned from the fact that even the upper bound estimate is well below one for all donors. That is, population increases are matched with less than proportional increases in the share of aid. Indeed, in the case of the US and the Arab donors, it cannot be said even with 90 per cent confidence that more aid goes to more populous countries.

One should not be too much worried about this population bias, however. As discussed in Chapter 3 there are various reasons for such a bias, not all of which are ethically dubious. Indeed, without a population bias the vast majority of aid would be concentrated in two countries only, namely China and India, by far the most populous of developing countries.

Recipient need

We have seen that donors do not take the physical quality of life into account in their aid allocation once income is controlled for. This holds true

Table 7.1 Statistical significance and estimated elasticity of the population variable

Donor	Eligibility stage	Level stage with 90% confidence interval		
		Lower bound	*Best estimate*	*Upper bound*
Total	n.a.	0.16	0.30	0.43
DAC	n.a.	0.19	0.34	0.49
Japan	n.a.	0.31	0.52	0.74
US	×	−0.22	0.00	0.22
Germany	n.a.	0.31	0.51	0.70
France	n.a.	0.38	0.53	0.68
UK	+	0.46	0.62	0.79
Italy	×	0.06	0.28	0.50
Canada	+	0.35	0.53	0.70
Denmark	+	0.02	0.25	0.48
The Netherlands	+	0.36	0.53	0.70
Norway	+	0.09	0.33	0.58
Sweden	+	0.23	0.45	0.68
Arab bilateral	+	−0.15	0.16	0.47
Arab multilateral	+	−0.01	0.13	0.28
Multilateral	n.a.	0.15	0.29	0.44
EC	n.a.	0.20	0.35	0.50
UN	n.a.	0.22	0.34	0.46
IDA	+	0.44	0.60	0.77

Notes
n.a. Not applicable.
×   Not significant.
+   Statistically significant with a positive sign.

both at the aid eligibility and the level stage. The only exceptions are Japan and the EC, for which this variable exerts the expected impact at the level stage. This represents a rather striking result: donors seem to be focused on economic, but not human development when they take the RN into account. Surprisingly, not even the like-minded donors provide an exception to this rule.

Given that income is the only variable of RN, which seems to matter, which donors are more sensitive towards the poverty of recipient countries than others? This question is answered in Table 7.2, which shows whether the income variable is statistically significant at the aid eligibility and level stages and compares the estimated income elasticity of aid allocation at the level stage across donors together with a 90 per cent confidence interval. It can be seen that the recipient country's poverty is a statistically significant determinant of aid eligibility for all donors. We can also be 90 per cent confident that most donors also give more aid to poorer countries at the

Table 7.2 Statistical significance and estimated elasticity of the income variable

Donor	Eligibility stage	Level stage with 90% confidence interval		
		Lower bound	*Best estimate*	*Upper bound*
Total	n.a.	−0.58	−0.86	−1.15
DAC	n.a.	−0.47	−0.80	−1.13
Japan	n.a.	−0.15	−0.50	−0.86
US	−	−0.04	−0.50	−0.96
Germany	n.a.	−0.46	−0.84	−1.23
France	n.a.	0.08	−0.22	−0.52
UK	−	−0.45	−0.90	−1.34
Italy	−	−0.43	−0.79	−1.15
Canada	−	−0.36	−0.71	−1.05
Denmark	−	0.16	−0.43	−1.02
The Netherlands	−	−0.57	−1.01	−1.45
Norway	−	−0.49	−0.91	−1.33
Sweden	−	−0.48	−1.25	−2.02
Arab bilateral	−	0.66	−0.13	−0.93
Arab multilateral	−	−0.12	−0.43	−0.74
Multilateral	n.a.	−0.84	−1.14	−1.44
EC	n.a.	−0.26	−0.56	−0.86
UN	n.a.	−0.52	−0.82	−1.12
IDA	−	−0.22	−0.51	−0.81

Notes
n.a. Not applicable.
−   Statistically significant with a negative sign.

level stage. The only exceptions are France, the Arab countries in their bilateral aid allocation and, surprisingly, Denmark. What about the middle-income bias discussed in Chapter 3? If we only look at the best estimate, then only the Dutch, Swedish and aggregate multilateral aid allocation are free of such bias as the estimated elasticity is bigger than one in absolute terms. However, if uncertainty in the estimations is taken into account, then it is only Japan, the US, France, the Arab bilateral donors, the EC and the IDA for which we can be 90 per cent confident that their aid allocation is characterised by a middle-income bias because even with the upper bound estimate proportional increases in income are associated with less than proportional decreases in the share of aid. Note that with respect to Japan and the EC one needs to treat this result with care as these are the only two donors, which also take the physical quality of life into account in their aid allocation, which suggests that RN plays more of a role in the aid allocation of these two donors than the estimated income elasticity would suggest. Also note that in accordance with the expectations, the estimated income elasticity is quite high for the like-minded countries. The only exception is Denmark. The coefficient of its income variable is measured so imprecisely, however, that the possibility that more aid goes to richer countries cannot be excluded. The possibility that not only does more aid go to poorer countries, but also that there is no middle-income bias cannot be excluded. This is because its lower bound estimate is positive, whereas its upper bound estimate is negative and bigger than one in absolute terms.

Donor interest

Table 7.3 provides an overview of the statistical significance of DI variables at the aid eligibility stage.[1] It is clear that DI by and large matters little at this stage. Former own colonies are fully eligible for Italian and US aid and are more likely to receive UK aid, but not Dutch aid. Three of the like-minded countries (Canada, the Netherlands and Norway) seem to give preference to recipient countries with a predominantly Christian population.

Donor interest matters much more at the level stage as the summary information contained in Table 7.4 shows. Military-strategic interests play a role at the aggregate bilateral, multilateral and total level. All the major donors with the exception of Germany and Italy also give more aid to countries, which receive a higher share of US military grants. Interestingly, even three of the like-minded donors do (Canada, Denmark and Norway). Colonial experience matters only where donors actually have had former colonies, whilst there is no such bias for the other donors. The only former colonial powers not to give more aid to their former colonies are Japan and

Table 7.3 Statistical significance of DI variables at eligibility stage

Donor	US military grants	Colonial experience	Political similarity	Exports	Religious similarity
US	×	Fully eligible	×	×	×
UK	×	+	×	×	×
Italy	×	Fully eligible	×	×	×
Canada	×	×	×	+	+
Denmark	×	×	×	×	×
The Netherlands	×	×	×	×	+
Norway	+	×	×	×	+
Sweden	×	×	×	×	×
IDA	×	×	×	×	−

Notes
× Not significant.
+ Statistically significant with a positive sign.
− Statistically significant with a negative sign.

Table 7.4 Statistical significance of DI variables at level stage

Donor	US military grants	Colonial experience	Exports	Political similarity	Religious similarity
Total	+	×	+	×	×
DAC	+	×	+	×	×
Japan	+	×	+	×	+
US	+	+	×	×	×
Germany	×	×	+	×	×
France	+	+	+	×	+
UK	+	+	×	×	×
Italy	×	+	×	×	+
Canada	+	×	+	×	×
Denmark	+	×	×	+	×
The Netherlands	×	+	−	×	×
Norway	+	×	×	×	×
Sweden	×	×	×	×	+
Multilateral	+	×	+	×	×
EC	×	×	×	+	×
UN	×	×	+	×	×
IDA	×	×	×	×	×

Notes
× Not significant.
+ Statistically significant with a positive sign.
− Statistically significant with a negative sign.

Germany. In the case of Japan, this is because of the traditionally difficult relationship between Japan and its former colonies. Their 'colonisation' consisted in occupation rather than Western-style colonisation. In the case of Germany, this donor lost all its colonies after the First World War such that the ties to these countries are less strong than the ones for the other former colonial powers. Economic DI in the form of exports also plays a role at the aggregate bilateral, multilateral and total level. The same is true for Germany and Japan, two major exporting nations, France (a strong promoter of its own interest) and Canada. In contrast to these 'hard' aspects of DIs, the 'soft' aspects such as political and religious similarity play a relatively small role.

Good governance

Table 7.5 provides an overview of the impact of GG on the aid eligibility stage. No consistent picture emerges with respect to any one donor, or group of donors or any one aspect of GG. Of all the aspects of GG, it seems that low regulatory burden is the one that plays the greatest role in that it

Table 7.5 Statistical significance of GG variables at eligibility stage

Donor	Democracy	Human rights	Low military expenditures	Low corruption	Rule of law	Low regulatory burden
US	+	×	×	×	−	+
UK	×	×	×	+	×	+
Italy	×	×	+	×	×	×
Canada	×	×	×	+	×	+
Denmark	×	+	+	×	×	+
The Netherlands	+	×	×	×	×	×
Norway	×	−	×	×	×	×
Sweden	×	×	×	×	×	×
Arab bilateral	×	×	+	×	×	×
Arab multilateral	+	+	×	−	×	+
IDA	×	+	×	×	×	+

Notes
× Not significant.
+ Statistically significant with a positive sign.
− Statistically significant with a negative sign.

represents a statistically significant determinant of the aid eligibility decisions of half of the donors. All other aspects assume statistical significance only for a few donors. Strikingly, there is no difference apparent between the like-minded countries and the rest of donors.

A similar picture emerges at the level stage, for which summary information is provided in Table 7.6. Low regulatory burden is again the aspect of GG that exerts a statistically significant positive impact upon the amount of aid given by quite a few donors and at the aggregate bilateral, multilateral and total level. Democracy is important for the aid allocation by Germany, Japan, the Netherlands, the US and at the aggregate bilateral level. Respect for human rights is statistically significant at the aggregate multilateral and total level, but at the disaggregated level only for Japan and the IDA. Low military expenditures are rewarded with higher aid flows from Germany, Canada, the Arab countries and the EC. Low corruption and respect for the rule of law are basically irrelevant. Again, no donor or group of donors stands out as a consistent promoter of GG. In particular, no difference is apparent between the like-minded countries and the rest of donors.

The relative substantive importance of variables

So far, the statistical significance of the variables have been mainly addressed. What about their substantive impact? In addressing this question

Table 7.6 Statistical significance of GG variables at level stage

Donor	Democracy	Human rights	Low military expenditures	Low corruption	Rule of law	Low regulatory burden
Total	×	+	×	×	×	+
DAC	+	×	×	×	−	+
Japan	+	+	×	−	×	+
US	+	×	×	×	×	×
Germany	+	×	+	×	×	×
France	×	×	×	×	×	×
UK	×	×	×	×	×	×
Italy	×	−	×	×	×	+
Canada	×	×	+	×	×	+
Denmark	×	×	×	×	×	×
The Netherlands	+	×	−	×	×	+
Norway	×	×	×	×	×	×
Sweden	×	×	×	+	×	×
Arab bilateral	×	×	+	×	×	×
Arab multilateral	×	×	×	×	×	×
Multilateral	×	+	×	×	×	+
EC	×	×	+	×	×	×
UN	×	×	×	×	×	×
IDA	×	+	×	×	×	×

Notes
× Not significant.
+ Statistically significant with a positive sign.
− Statistically significant with a negative sign.

the level stage is concentrated upon, as for quite a few donors this is the only relevant stage. Which variables are more important than others at the level stage? Unfortunately, this question has no easy and indeed no definite answer. This is because one cannot simply compare the magnitude of estimated coefficients as the variables are held in different units. To do so would be tantamount to comparing apples with oranges. Indeed, because variables are held in different units there is no definite way of comparing the substantive importance of variables (King 1986). What will be done below is to compare percentage increases in the share of aid following a one standard deviation increase or decrease in one of the explanatory variables. This is the method of (semi)-standardised coefficients and it gives some feeling for the relative importance of variables, but there are other ways one can think of that could lead to somewhat different results. The reason why a one standard deviation change is looked at rather than a percentage or absolute change in the explanatory variable is to compare aid increases following a relatively substantive change in the explanatory variable. What such a relatively substantive change is depends on the distribution of a variable and is therefore better captured by a one standard deviation change than by a percentage change or a change in absolute terms.

Table 7.7 presents the estimated percentage increase in the share of aid a country receives due to a one standard deviation decrease in income. In addition to the best estimate, a 90 per cent confidence interval is also stated. Countries are sorted in descending order according to the best estimate.

It is not surprising to see three like-minded donors and aggregate multilateral aid flows to be the top four in terms of sensitivity of the aid allocation towards recipient country's poverty. A one standard deviation decrease in income is followed by a 116 per cent increase in the share of Swedish aid as the best estimate. One can be 90 per cent confident that the true value lies between a lower bound of 44 per cent and an upper bound of 187 per cent. It can be seen that for most donors a one standard deviation decrease in the recipient country's income is followed by quite substantial increases in the share of aid. In looking at the lower bound estimate, it can also be seen that only in the case of Denmark, France and the Arab countries there cannot be 90 per cent confidence that more aid is given to poorer countries as already seen in Table 7.2.

Table 7.7 Per cent increase in aid share following a one standard deviation decrease in income (90% confidence interval)

Country	Lower bound	Best estimate	Upper bound
Sweden	44.07	115.52	186.99
Multilateral	78.17	105.92	133.66
The Netherlands	52.54	93.33	134.12
Norway	45.42	84.30	123.17
UK	41.32	82.91	124.44
Total	53.41	79.81	106.20
Germany	42.64	78.23	113.82
UN	48.17	75.96	103.75
DAC	43.55	74.23	104.93
Italy	39.69	73.16	106.57
Canada	33.91	65.42	96.93
EC	23.98	51.57	79.16
IDA	20.48	47.61	74.74
Japan	13.81	46.67	79.53
US	4.05	46.38	88.70
Arab multilateral	11.52	39.92	68.30
Denmark	−14.76	39.71	94.19
France	−7.67	20.08	47.83
Arab bilateral	−61.06	12.37	85.81

How do the DI variables compare? We concentrate on the three variables, which the prior chapters have revealed to be the ones most often statistically significant: former colonial experience, imports and US military grants. Table 7.8 shows the estimated percentage increase in the aid share following a one standard deviation increase in the share of US military grants, in the share of exports from the donor(s) and in the years of former colonial experience.[2] As concerns colonial status, it is clear that both France and the UK reward a one standard deviation increase in former colonial experience with very substantial increases in the share of aid: about 190 per cent in the case of France and for British aid about 120 per cent. The UK and France, in particular, are well known for colonial bias in their aid allocation. In the case of Dutch aid allocation, the respective increase in the share of aid is merely about one-third of the UK one. It is about one-fifth in the case of Italy and becomes smaller still in the case of US aid allocation. With German and Japanese aid, we even cannot be confident that more aid goes to their former colonies. The same is true for all donors without own former colonies: general former colonial experience by a Western or EU country does not lead to statistically significantly more aid receipt. A one standard deviation increase in the share of donors' exports increases the aid share between about 15 and 45 per cent for most donors as the best estimate, with Japan standing out at about 75 per cent. It is not surprising to find that the two major exporting nations among Western donors (Japan and Germany) are at the top of this list. A one standard deviation increase in the share of US military grants leads to a comparatively small increase in the share of aid. The best estimate is below 10 per cent for all donors and even the upper bound estimate is always below 15 per cent. It is not surprising to find the US among the top of the list, but is surprising to find Denmark and aggregate multilateral aid flows there. On the very top of the list is again Japan. This might come as a surprise given that Japan is no major Western military power. Its army is relatively small and it does not export arms to any significant extent. However, it has often been observed that exactly for this reason Japan is willing to provide substantial support for Western military-strategic interests in its aid allocation as a substitute for its minor military role (Katada 1997), which is what we observe here.

By and large, it is seen that the extent of poverty in recipient countries is a substantively important determinant of aid allocation and often more important than either colonial status, exports or US military grants on their own, with the exception of France and the UK (colonial status) and Japan (exports). However, as there are various aspects of DI, they need to be regarded together of course and then both RN and DI are of roughly similar importance for most donors with variations according to expectations: For the like-minded donors RN by and large is more important as

Table 7.8 Per cent increase in aid share following a one standard deviation increase in DI variables (90% confidence interval)

US military grants

Country	Lower bound	Best estimate	Upper bound
Japan	5.00	8.43	11.94
Multilateral	2.98	8.23	13.75
US	1.90	7.90	14.25
Denmark	4.03	7.50	11.04
UK	0.19	7.20	14.63
Canada	0.37	6.97	13.96
Total	4.29	6.05	7.86
DAC	4.07	5.98	7.93
France	0.87	5.88	11.11
Norway	1.93	5.62	9.41
The Netherlands	-2.50	3.33	9.54
IDA	-0.15	2.69	5.65
Germany	-2.47	0.78	4.16
Sweden	-5.15	0.59	6.70
UN	-2.77	-0.37	2.03
Italy	-11.79	-2.89	6.87
EC	-16.79	-4.88	8.70

Exports

Country	Lower bound	Best estimate	Upper bound
Japan	45.05	75.45	105.81
DAC	19.96	44.01	68.08
Germany	14.69	43.49	72.27
Total	13.46	34.89	56.34
France	19.04	33.63	48.19
UN	15.60	33.01	50.35
US	-0.63	30.97	62.62
Canada	5.87	25.02	44.15
Multilateral	3.18	24.34	45.52
Denmark	-14.18	17.99	50.19
Norway	-9.78	17.16	44.10
UK	-7.74	16.88	41.51
Italy	-10.80	15.86	42.54
EC	-7.62	9.79	27.22
Sweden	-48.75	-15.91	16.90
IDA	-57.19	-27.61	1.97
The Netherlands	-51.65	-32.47	-13.30

Colonial experience

Country	Lower bound	Best estimate	Upper bound
France	149.52	188.45	232.80
UK	80.71	120.99	169.60
The Netherlands	8.86	44.39	91.63
Denmark	-2.17	35.16	86.75
Italy	16.44	26.71	37.61
EC	-15.24	21.32	49.65
US	10.13	16.44	23.08
Canada	-7.48	14.11	40.75
Germany	-5.27	10.26	28.41
UN	-8.25	4.06	18.03
DAC	-16.11	0.35	20.03
Norway	-28.22	-1.86	34.19
Total	-17.44	-2.79	14.47
Multilateral	-19.29	-5.62	10.36
Japan	-19.50	-8.39	4.24
IDA	-20.96	-9.54	3.53
Sweden	-45.35	-22.38	10.24

Table 7.9 Per cent increase in aid share following a one standard deviation improvement in GG variables (90% confidence interval)

Respect for human rights

Country	Lower bound	Best estimate	Upper bound
Japan	19.11	35.35	53.81
IDA	4.05	19.12	36.34
Multilateral	6.25	16.24	27.21
Sweden	−6.26	16.24	44.15
Arab multilateral	−4.40	10.85	28.56
UK	−4.62	7.78	21.78
Total	0.62	7.65	15.16
Germany	−4.33	5.04	15.35
EC	−7.40	4.41	17.75
DAC	−3.70	4.32	13.02
France	−6.10	2.90	12.76
Norway	−11.78	0.79	15.16
Arab bilateral	−33.83	−0.33	50.13
US	−14.81	−3.20	10.00
The Netherlands	−18.95	−5.41	10.39
UN	−11.56	−5.46	1.05
Denmark	−22.14	−7.15	19.01
Canada	−22.34	−11.48	0.89
Italy	−28.13	−15.73	−1.19

Democracy

Country	Lower bound	Best estimate	Upper bound
US	14.98	34.56	53.59
The Netherlands	5.87	31.55	63.46
Japan	7.13	28.88	55.03
Denmark	−11.56	16.83	54.39
EC	−0.35	15.94	34.98
Arab multilateral	−7.69	14.90	43.06
Germany	2.64	13.86	26.26
DAC	2.86	13.39	24.99
Multilateral	−4.19	11.20	29.15
France	−2.47	9.81	23.65
Total	−0.52	9.32	20.21
UK	−6.07	9.24	27.14
Canada	−5.88	8.79	25.78
Italy	−15.15	5.98	32.42
Arab bilateral	−44.04	−7.69	52.15
IDA	−18.45	−7.76	4.34
Norway	−25.42	−8.62	11.97
Sweden	−27.35	−10.16	11.04
The Netherlands	−51.65	−32.47	−13.30

Low regulatory burden

Country	Lower bound	Best estimate	Upper bound
Japan	89.75	157.34	248.99
Canada	18.26	60.27	117.19
The Netherlands	1.21	58.52	148.08
Total	21.92	54.12	94.85
DAC	15.49	51.89	99.78
Italy	6.78	44.80	96.41
Multilateral	12.62	40.64	75.66
US	−12.57	34.93	108.28
Arab bilateral	−40.16	26.32	166.54
Germany	−12.00	25.18	78.08
UK	−17.03	19.48	72.08
Arab multilateral	−10.55	18.37	56.64
IDA	−16.95	17.33	65.76
France	−13.10	14.37	50.54
EC	−15.15	9.64	41.68
UN	−15.99	1.88	23.57
Norway	−37.37	−5.45	42.72
Denmark	−51.05	−23.37	19.94
Sweden	−55.08	−26.80	19.28

they do not reward former colonial experience (with the exception of the Netherlands) and mostly do not use aid allocation for export promotion.

How do the variables of GG compare? As with DI, we will concentrate on the three variables, which prior chapters have found to be the ones more often statistically significant than the others. Results are presented in Table 7.9. With 90 per cent confidence more aid goes to countries with a one standard deviation increase in respect for human rights only for few donors. Even where this is the case, the resultant increase in the share of aid is below 20 per cent, apart from Japan where 35 per cent is our best estimate. A one standard deviation improvement in democracy is rewarded with increases in the share of aid received of about similar magnitude. This time, the US tops the list of donors, which is not surprising given the traditional emphasis on electoral democracy in US foreign aid allocation and indeed US foreign policy more generally. Relatively more important than either respect for human rights or democracy is the regulatory burden imposed on the recipient country's economy. Japan is again at the top of the list, rewarding a one standard deviation decrease in such burden by a 157 per cent higher share of aid, which is almost three times higher than that of Canada. As with DI, one best looks at these various aspects of GG together. The best estimates suggest that GG need not be much less of substantive importance than either RN or DI *if donors consistently rewarded all aspects of GG*. However, the problem is that for most donors most of the GG variables do not assume statistical significance such that we cannot be 90 per cent confident that they actually do give more aid to recipient countries that perform well on this aspect of GG. Indeed, Japan is the only donor for which we can be 90 per cent confident that it gives more aid to recipient countries with greater respect for human rights, greater extent of democracy and lower regulatory burden. For many other donors, we can have such confidence only for one or the other aspect of GG and for some donors GG does not seem to play any role at all. Because of this lack of consistency, GG is clearly less important for the allocation of aid than either RN or DI is. Another striking result is that the like-minded countries do not generally fare better than the other donors. Whilst Sweden is among the top as concerns democracy, it is at the very bottom as concerns respect for human rights and low regulatory burden. Denmark is among the top as concerns respect for human rights, but at the bottom for the other two aspects of GG. Canada is among the top as concerns regulatory burden, but not for respect for human rights or democracy. Norway is at the bottom for respect for human rights and low regulatory burden and in the lower half for democracy. Only the Netherlands is in the top for two aspects of GG, but it is also in the bottom as concerns democracy. Clearly, the like-minded donors do not stand out as promoters of GG – not as single countries and not as a group either.

8   Testing the robustness of results

In this chapter, the results from the preceding chapters are subjected to a number of sensitivity checks. It starts with a consideration of changes to the specification of models and then turns to the so-called endogeneity problem.

Results are robust to changes in model specification

The results reported in earlier chapters and summarised in the last chapter suggest that GG does not exert a consistent or substantively important role in the allocation of aid in the 1990s. The results are robust with respect to a number of changes. They do not change dramatically if:

- The time-invariant indicators of the extent of corruption and respect for the rule of law from the World Bank data set are replaced by their time-varying counterparts from the international-country risk guide (ICRG) data set. The latter were not used in the main analysis as they are available for fewer countries than the World Bank variables.
- The Cingranelli and Richards (1999) measure of respect for human rights is used in lieu of the respective measure from Gibney's (2002) Political Terror Scales (PTS). Again, the reason why the data from the PTS is used again is due to the lower availability of the Cingranelli and Richards (1999) data.
- The variables of GG are included in the model to be estimated in isolation rather than in combination. This suggests, as discussed already in Chapter 4, that multicollinearity is not responsible for the fact that often aspects of GG are insignificant.
- The models are estimated with Heckman's sample selection model rather than the two-part model.

What all this means is that the results are not an artefact of the particular model specification, but provide a valid analysis of the impact that GG has (or, as it happens, often does not have) on aid allocation by the major donors.

The endogeneity problem: does more aid really go to poorer countries and major importers?

In Chapter 4, it has been mentioned that the two-part model has important practical advantages. One of these, which is made use of in this chapter, is that it is easier to deal with another problem in the data, namely the (potential) endogeneity of some of the explanatory variables. Endogeneity of an explanatory variable implies that it is correlated with the error term. If existent, it will bias the estimation of the coefficients of the explanatory variables and, importantly, not just of the endogenous variables, but of all explanatory variables, including the truly exogenous ones.

Endogeneity can represent a problem due to the existence of omitted variables, measurement error or simultaneity. Omitted variables are variables that are determinants of the dependent variable, but they are not controlled for in the estimation either because they were not included or, more importantly, they cannot be measured. If the omitted variables are correlated with the included explanatory variables, then the latter will be correlated with the error term as by definition omitted variables are part of the error term due to their omission. Measurement error refers to errors in the measurement of the explanatory variables. Again, if existent, the explanatory variables will be correlated with the error term as the measurement error enters the error term of the equation to be estimated. These two reasons for endogeneity are generally important, but for the purpose of the analysis we will be concerned only with the third reason, namely simultaneity. We do so on the assumption that any important variables in the estimations has not been omitted and that any apparent measurement error is too insignificant to cause substantial problems. As will be seen, simultaneity on the other hand is a cause for potential endogeneity bias that cannot simply be neglected in the context of explaining the pattern of aid allocation.

Simultaneity exists if some of the explanatory variables are determined simultaneously with the dependent variable. This is the case if, for example, some of the explanatory variables are functions of the dependent variable. This poses the greatest concern in terms of endogeneity in the context. Of course, some of the explanatory variables can truly be regarded as exogenous, for example, former colonial experience and the religious composition of a country. Others are potentially endogenous, but it is justified to assume that, for example, voting similarity in the UN general assembly and the quality of governance are reasonably exogenous. The two variables that simply cannot uphold the assumption of exogeneity are income per capita and exports to recipient countries. It is easy to see why. With respect to exports, there is both qualitative and quantitative evidence that aid is given with the intention and often the result of spurring donor exports (see, e.g. Lloyd *et al.* (2000, 2001)). Also, often aid is tied to procurement of goods from the donor country, which will imply more exports from the donor to the recipient country. The potential endogeneity of the income variable is even more obvious. After all, the ultimate goal of aid donation is to raise income levels in recipient countries. In addition, the PQLI variable also suffers from potential endogeneity bias for the same reason the income variable does. However, given that this variable is highly insignificant in the aid allocation of most donors and that it becomes more difficult to control for endogeneity the more potentially endogenous variables are included, the PQLI variable was dropped from the estimations – see discussion further below.

Simultaneity is a problem that is routinely ignored in the aid allocation literature even though it was raised already by Mosley (1980) in his critique of the McKinlay and Little (1977, 1978a,b) studies. The endogeneity problem is tackled with the help of instrumental variables (IV). Such IV need to fulfil two conditions: first, they must not be endogenous since otherwise they would suffer from the very same problem they are supposed to remedy. Second, they need to be partially correlated with the endogenous variables in the sense that the correlation persists after all other exogenous variables are controlled for (Wooldridge 2002: 84). The stronger the correlation the better. IV estimation effectively rules out endogeneity bias in that only that part of the endogenous variables is used in the estimation of the equation of interest that is uncorrelated with the error term and therefore exogenous. This is achieved in regressing each endogenous variable on all exogenous variables plus the IV, using the fitted values and correcting the standard errors in a procedure called two-stage least squares (2SLS) estimation. Another practical advantage of being able to employ the two-part model can now be seen. It is clear that to deal with endogeneity problems with the help of IV estimation is much easier in this model due to its separate estimations of the equations explaining aid eligibility and the level stage allocation of aid. Again, whilst it is not impossible to estimate, there is no routine available for IV estimation in Heckman's sample selection model, at least not in Stata®.

But how can one know that the instruments used fulfil the two conditions for IVs stated above? The second condition, the partial correlation with the endogenous variables, is relatively easy to check and the instruments used, which will be described later on, fulfil this condition. The first condition required that the instruments themselves are not endogenous. This condition can in principle be tested if one has what is called over-identifying restrictions. Loosely speaking, this means that one has more instruments than endogenous variables to be instrumented. In other words, one has more instruments than are needed for identification, one has more than just identified, and has over-identified the equation to be estimated. The test of over-identifying restrictions works in comparing the IV estimation results for the just identified to the over-identified equation. If the two estimations do not systematically differ then one can have some statistical confidence that the instruments are truly exogenous. As we will see further below, we have over-identifying restrictions so that can we apply the test.

In deriving the instruments our analysis mainly follows the 'geography hypothesis' explanation of cross-country differences in income levels and the quality of life, which relates such differences to geographic, climatic or ecological differences across countries (see, e.g. Gallup *et al.* 1999; McArthur and Sachs 2001). We note that there is a competing 'institutional hypothesis', which explains income and quality of life differences with reference to the institutional organisation of societies (see, e.g. Sokoloff and Engerman 2000; Easterly 2001; Engerman *et al.* 2001; Acemoglu *et al.* 2001a,b). In my view the contest between the two hypotheses is unresolved. More importantly, I believe that the major difference between these two competing hypothesis is founded in the exact mechanism through which geography affects income, but that both hypotheses in the end refer to geographical factors as the source of explaining variation in cross-country income levels. For example, Acemoglu *et al.* (2001a) suggest that where European settlers were confronted with high mortality rates in the colonised tropical areas, they were less likely to settle and more likely to install 'extractive' institutions. These are institutions whose major purpose is the extraction of resources and the transfer of wealth to the colonial power rather than domestic economic development. Engerman *et al.* (2001) argue that colonies in tropical ecozones were conducive to growing crops such as sugarcane that promoted the use of slave labour, creating enormous inequalities and a drag on economic development.

For the purpose of this chapter, the exact way in which geography affects income levels does not matter so much. The instruments put forward by the 'geography hypothesis' are used mainly since they are available for many more countries than the main IV used by the 'institutional hypothesis' (European settler mortality in the seventeenth, eighteenth and nineteenth century). However, some variables that follow more from the 'institutional hypothesis' have been used as well. The following set of instruments has been used:

• A country's share of land area located in the geographical tropics. The absence of frost days leads to higher disease burdens (particularly malaria) and lower agricultural productivity, which hinders the development of tropical countries (Gallup *et al.* 1999; Masters and

McMillan 2001). More highly developed countries are, all other things equal, also more likely to import more Western goods and services. Data are taken from Gallup *et al.* (1999) and were extended for the many small countries missing with the help of the Koppen-Geiger climatological map of the world (Geiger and Pohl 1954).

- A country's absolute latitude. For climatic reasons European settlers tended to settle away from the equator. The extent of historic settlement by Europeans is highly correlated with economic development as the settlers brought with them their skills, technology and institutions conducive to economic development. Data are taken from Parker (1997) and La Porta *et al.* (1999).

- A dummy variable, which was set to one if a country is a net exporter of fossil fuels and zero otherwise. Data are taken from World Bank (2000). A country that is a net exporter of fossil fuels can, all other things equal, enjoy a higher per capita income and will have more foreign exchange to finance imports of Western goods and services. Whilst the amount of aid given might have an influence on the exact amount of fossil fuels extracted, the net fossil fuel export position is predominantly determined by geological factors and is *not* endogenous to aid giving.

In dealing with the endogeneity problem, the level stage will be focussed upon, which is the more important and the more susceptible one to endogeneity problems. The analysis is confined to a comparison of the statistical significance and the sign of the coefficient of the instrumented variables. The variables, which were not instrumented, are generally little affected by the IV estimations and are therefore not reported here. The reason why the magnitude of the estimated coefficients are ignored even though the IV estimates are usually greater in size than the non-IV estimates is that they are also more imprecise such that one cannot really be confident that the estimated effect is bigger with IV estimation than without it. The statistical significance and sign of the income and exports variables are compared from non-IV to IV estimations with the PQLI variable dropped from the model. The reason for this is to enhance the efficiency of IV estimation. The estimates become more precise with fewer variables to be instrumented, particularly if they are correlated with each other as is the case with income and the PQLI. Also, with only three instruments available it would be impossible to test for over-identifying restrictions if there were three variables that needed instrumentation. Given that the PQLI variable has been estimated as highly insignificant for most donors' aid allocation in previous chapters, it is justified to run IV estimations with this variable dropped from the estimations. If the PQLI variable is included as well, then estimations become so inefficient that in most cases all three variables (PQLI, income and exports) are simply insignificant.

Table 8.1 compares the statistical significance and the coefficient sign of the income and exports variables from the non-IV estimation results with results from Baltagi's random-effects IV estimator where the instruments are as described further above. Note that because the IV estimator has no robust option, the reported IV results necessarily refer to non-robust standard errors and for consistency reasons the non-IV results are reported without robust standard errors as well. This together with the fact that the PQLI variable has been dropped from the model means that the non-IV results reported in Table 8.1 are very similar, but not identical, to the ones reported in earlier chapters.

It can be seen that a country's poverty as measured by its per capita income remains a statistically significant determinant of the level of aid

Table 8.1 Comparison of IV results with non-IV results

Donor	Non-IV results		IV results		Test of over-identifying restrictions	
	Income	*Exports*	*Income*	*Exports*	*chi²*	*p-value*
Total	−	+	−	+	0.78	0.377
DAC	−	+	−	+	0.99	0.319
Japan	−	+	−	+	0.10	0.748
US	−	+	−	+	4.50	0.034
Germany	−	+	−	×	0.18	0.668
France	−	+	−	+	0.52	0.472
UK	−	×	−	×	2.46	0.117
Italy	−	×	−	+	2.01	0.157
Canada	−	+	−	+	0.79	0.375
Denmark	×	×	−	+	1.54	0.215
The Netherlands	−	−	−	×	1.89	0.169
Norway	−	×	−	×	0.00	0.960
Sweden	−	×	−	+	0.32	0.571
Arab bilateral	×	×	×	×	0.38	0.539
Arab multilateral	−	×	×	×	2.38	0.123
Multilateral	−	+	−	+	0.53	0.466
EC	−	×	−	+	0.01	0.919
UN	−	+	−	×	2.31	0.129
IDA	−	×	−	×	0.28	0.594

Notes
× Not significant.
+ Statistically significant with a positive sign.
− Statistically significant with a negative sign.

allocation by most donors once the endogeneity is controlled for. Arab multilateral aid allocation is the only one for which non-IV estimation suggests a statistically significant effect of the income variable, but not the IV estimation. Danish aid allocation, on the other hand, which was insensitive towards a recipient country's income level in non-IV estimation, gives more aid to poorer countries once the endogeneity is controlled for. Results for the export variable are not quite as consistent. It is statistically insignificant in non-IV estimation, but assumes statistical significance in IV estimation in the case of Italian, Danish, Swedish and EC aid allocation. The IV estimation results for these are more in line with the expectations. The export variable is statistically significant in non-IV, but not in IV estimation in the case of Germany, the Netherlands and the UN agencies. The Dutch case is least worrisome as the non-IV effect was with a sign contrary to expectation anyway. In the case of UN agencies, it was somewhat surprising to find a statistically significant positive effect of the export variable in non-IV estimation given that Western countries' exporting interests should have little influence on the allocation of aid by the UN. More troublesome is the result for German aid allocation as it suggests that Germany, one of the major exporting nations, does not pursue its exporting interests in aid giving once the potential endogeneity of the export variable is controlled for. It is unclear whether the insignificance of the export variable is caused by actual insignificance or highly inefficient IV estimation. The results from the tests of over-identifying restrictions clearly suggest the exogeneity of the IVs for all donors but the US, in which case the test marginally rejects the exogeneity hypothesis. What this means is that the variables are valid instruments for use in the IV estimation.

In sum, the IV estimations provide evidence that on the whole the prior results do not suffer too much from endogeneity bias. The basic results still hold true: practically all donors give more aid to poorer countries and more aid goes to the major importers of goods and services by the major donors, some like-minded countries as well as to the major importers of Western goods in the case of aggregate aid flows.

9 Conclusions

The results from the analysis of the pattern of aid allocation in the 1990s can be summarised as follows:

- Most donors give preference to more populous countries at the aid eligibility stage and give more aid to more populous countries at the level stage, but at this stage all donors share a bias against more populous countries in so far as they receive less aid *per capita* than less populous ones.
- All donors give preference to poorer countries at the aid eligibility stage. At the level stage, most donors share a middle-income bias if one looks at the best estimate of the income elasticity. If uncertainty is taken into account, then for the majority of donors one can no longer be 90 per cent confident that there is a bias against very poor countries.
- The physical quality of life does not exert a statistically significant impact upon aid allocation once income is controlled for. In other words, almost all donors regard income to be the relevant aspect of RN. As it seems, the donors' focus is on economic development, not human development need.
- Donor interest plays hardly any role at the aid eligibility stage. Former colonial powers often select their own colonies with greater probability, however.
- The 'hard' aspects of DI are often statistically significant determinants at the level stage: colonial experience, economic interests in the form of exports and military-strategic interests. The like-minded donors are not entirely free of such influence. In comparison, the rather 'soft' aspects of DI hardly matter at all (political similarity) or only for a few donors (religious similarity).
- All aspects of GG with the exception of respect for the rule of law exert some statistically significant influence upon the aid eligibility stage. However, such influence is confined to a few donors and no donor

consistently selects recipient countries with good performance on the various aspects of GG with greater probability.

- Democracy, respect for human rights, low military expenditures and low regulatory burden are statistically significant determinants at the level stage for some donors. However, as at the eligibility stage no donor consistently gives more aid to recipient countries with good performance on the various aspects of GG.
- Of the various aspects of GG, low regulatory burden is the one that assumes statistical significance in more cases than the other aspects at both the aid eligibility and the level stage.
- Recipient need and DI are of roughly similar substantive importance at the level stage. In accordance with expectation, RN is somewhat more important for most like-minded countries than DI is.
- Where aspects of GG are statistically significant determinants of aid allocation at the level stage, their combined substantive importance compares well with that of RN and DI. The problem is that usually only one or the other aspect of GG is statistically significant and in isolation aspects of GG are substantively less important than RN or DI, even where they are statistically significant. The only exception is low regulatory burden whose substantive importance is quite strong.
- There is no difference apparent between any one like-minded country or the like-minded countries as a group and the rest of donors in terms of statistical significance of GG on either stage. GG is also not of higher substantive importance for the like-minded countries than for the other donors.
- Major results are robust towards a range of sensitivity checks including controlling for the potential endogeneity of the income and exports variables.

How do these results compare with existing studies? No direct comparison is possible since the period of study is more recent than almost any other study and since we control for many more aspects of GG than any existing study. Having said this, the population bias and the often found middle-income bias is in accordance with the existing literature. So is the finding that the 'hard' aspects of DI matter most (colonial experience, exports, military-strategic interests). Like Tsoutsoplides (1991) I find that more EC aid goes to countries with a low PQLI, but also that the same is not true for most other aid flows. These similarities in findings are comforting as they suggest that the results with respect to the impact of GG on aid allocation in the 1990s are valid and not caused by the specific model specifications.

The results with respect to the variables of GG are more difficult to compare with existing studies since few studies have addressed GG and none has included a similarly comprehensive set of variables. That the extent of corruption has no impact upon aid allocation is congruent with similar findings by Alesina and Weder (2000), Svensson (2000) and Neumayer (2003a). That democracy and respect for human rights have some impact upon aggregate aid flows is in accordance with Neumayer (2003b). That the UN agencies do not stand out as promoters of GG in their aid allocation is in line with Neumayer (2003a). Contrary to some prior work by, for example, Cingranelli and Pasquarello (1985), Abrams and Lewis (1993), Poe (1992), Poe *et al.* (1994) and Apodaca and Stohl (1999) we do not find that US aid allocation takes respect for personal integrity rights into account. The major drawback of these studies is that they either do not control for democracy or combine democracy and respect for personal integrity rights into one measure. Our estimations control for democracy and respect for personal integrity rights separately. The results suggest that the US takes into account democracy in its aid allocation, but not respect for personal integrity rights, and that these earlier studies mistakenly attribute an effect to personal integrity rights that is actually due to democracy.

One striking result of this study is that a difference between the like-minded countries, which have a reputation of putting emphasis on GG, and the other donors is not found. This result is in accordance with Neumayer (2003c), but stands in contrast to Svensson (1999) who finds a difference between the like-minded countries and the big aid donors as concerns the impact of democracy on the level of aid allocated. However, since he fails to control for any variables of DI and for aspects of GG other than democracy, I have little faith in his results. Like Alesina and Dollar (2000) I find that more democratic countries receive more aid from Germany, Japan, the Netherlands and the US. However, I fail to find evidence for such an effect in the case of Canada, the Scandinavian countries and the UK. Alesina and Dollar (2000) control for variables of DI so the reason for the difference in results must lie somewhere else. Partly it might be explained by the fact that we control for more aspects of GG and the democracy variable might assume statistical significance in Alesina and Dollar (2000) for another variable of GG with which democracy is correlated. Alternatively, the reason could lie in the different time period of study even though it is difficult to see why democracy should play less of a role in the allocation of aid in the 1990s compared to the period of 1970–1994 of Alesina and Dollar's (2000) study.

Pronk (2001: 624) seems to suggest that many donors now follow the selectivity strategy in the pursuit of promoting GG. Collier (1997: 59), on the other hand, suggests that there is very little selectivity in aid allocation. The analysis has shown that there is selectivity only to some limited extent, thus confirming more Collier's than Pronk's view. There is not a single donor, which would consistently select countries with good performance across various aspects of GG with higher probability or would give more aid to such countries. If selectivity is followed it is followed inconsistently. This is true for individual donors, in that some aspect of GG is rewarded, but not others. Being consistent would imply to promote all aspects of GG comprehensively. Inconsistency also holds across donors. The aspect of GG, which plays a role for one donor often is irrelevant for another donor. If donors do not want to promote all aspects of GG, then the least they need to do is to find a consensus on which aspect to promote consistently across donors.

Interestingly, even those donors, which have more vigorously eschewed the selectivity strategy verbally, such as the Netherlands, do not seem to stick consistently to this strategy in their actual aid allocation. One might object that the analysis covers the whole decade of the 1990s, whereas the Dutch commitment to a selectivity strategy is of a more recent nature. However, Hout (2002) finds that the list of countries selected by the Dutch government after 1998 for receiving its major aid 'is almost impossible to replicate (...) with the help of reputable governance data-sets', which are similar to the ones used in this analysis. The only variable with some explanatory power is the regulatory burden on the economy. This is of course exactly the same variable that has been found to be of statistical significance more often than any other aspect of GG and of greatest substantive importance as well.

It is somewhat ironic that the aspect of GG that is relatively more important than the other ones turns out to be low regulatory burden. This is because it is also the aspect of GG, which is more contestable than the other ones as it eschews a particular neoclassical view of what is good economic management. Interestingly, even some of the like-minded donors seem to subscribe to this view. The other aspects, which are much less contestable, such as democracy, respect for human rights, low military expenditures, low corruption and respect for the rule of law are comparatively less important.

We are not the first ones to doubt the real commitment of the like-minded donors with respect to the promotion of GG. As Gillies (1999: 258) points out, their reputation as staunch defenders of GG in general and human rights in particular mainly derives from such things as roll-call diplomacy in UN fora and other actions that are relatively costless to the country. In his more qualitative and case-study analysis he finds that once more assertive channels are considered, which are more costly to the executing country, then 'the reputation of Canada, the Netherlands and Norway as human rights entrepreneurs is not as convincing as is commonly supposed'. As this quantitative study has shown, the same applies to aspects of GG other than human rights as well and indeed also to all the other like-minded countries.

In Chapter 4 it has been argued that if donors want to promote GG in recipient countries as they claim they do, then selectivity in aid allocation would be an appropriate strategy for achieving this aim together with assistance for capacity building. We have found only limited evidence that donors apply the selectivity strategy. It cannot be concluded that donors are, therefore, guilty of hypocrisy as they might promote GG in recipient countries via other channels not captured by the quantitative analysis of the allocation of aid flows. However, proof of this is yet to be seen. As mentioned in Chapter 4, there is some evidence that some donors and the like-minded countries in particular provide money with the specific purpose of capacity building for the improvement of governance. However, it has also been seen there that these funds are also very limited compared to general aid giving. In any case, I agree strongly with Hout (2002: 524) who finds it disconcerting that 'money is spent on countries which, according to the intended criteria, do not deserve it, while deserving countries are excluded'. If donors want to promote GG, then they need to resort to the selectivity strategy much more consistently and vigorously in the twenty-first century than they seem to have done in the last decade of the twentieth century.

Notes

1 Introduction

1 Note that this does not include Arab money to other non-Arab multilateral donors such as the UN, for example.

2 Good governance and its relation to aid

1 Indeed, as Theobald (1997: 301) points out, at least for Africa and despite the rhetoric to the contrary, conditionality has always focused more on economic rather than political aspects. Bad governance is as much a political as an economic problem, however.

4 Research design

1 Ironically, Maddala (1985, 1992) suggests that the type I Tobit model is inappropriate even for Tobin's (1958) original problem, but we cannot pursue this point further here.

2 Note, however, that contrary to the type I Tobit model, the two-part model in its general form is not a specific case of the type II Tobit model.

3 There is a further disadvantage to the two-part model that should at least be mentioned, even if it is of no further relevance in the context. Whilst the sample selection model can predict the unconditional or potential outcome as well as the conditional or actual outcome, the two-part model can only do the latter. In this context only the conditional outcome is of interest, that is, the amount of aid allocated conditional on the sample of countries eligible for aid receipt. Things are different in different contexts, however, for example, if the returns to education are to be estimated. Even though only the wages of those in employment are observed, the unconditional outcome is also of interest, that is, the return to education for all people that have received education, not just those that are in paid employment.

4 According to Breen (1996: 45), it is not unusual to find studies that come to similar conclusions about the independence of both estimations.

5 Alternatively, a logit estimator could have been used. Logit and probit lead to very similar results in standard situations.

6 Ideally, they would have wanted to estimate the grant equivalent of technical assistance, but saw themselves unable to do so.

7 The Pearson correlation coefficient is 0.88 for aggregate bilateral flows and 0.91 for multilateral flows.

8 Note that there is a whole group of political entities, namely dependent territories of donor countries, for which practically no explanatory variables would exist since they usually are collected for sovereign nation states only. The exclusion of dependent territories from the sample is not a problem, however, since aid going to these entities is conceptually different in being closer to intra-national transfers than cross-national financial flows and likely to be ruled by different determinants than aid going to sovereign countries.

9 The HDI, first introduced by UNDP (1990) and then developed over the years in its annual Human Development Reports, is also a composite indicator comprising income (which is heavily discounted above the world average income), life expectancy at birth and a combination of adult literacy and the combined first-, second- and third-level gross educational enrolment ratio.

10 For a comprehensive analysis of the relativist challenge to human rights, see Perry (1997).

11 See, for example, San Suu Kyi (1995) and Moon and Dixon (1992).

12 The reader should note that such high correlation is just an initial hint that multicollinearity might pose a problem, but not conclusive evidence by any means (see Maddala 2000).

13 The same applies to other aspects of governance covered by this dataset – see p. 55.

6 The Arab donors

1 Note, however, that towards the end of the 1990s the aid to GNI ratios have fallen to an all time low and even below the average DAC figures (Neumayer 2003e).

2 Arab countries are the major, but not the only, providers of money for the Islamic Development Bank.

3 Things are slowly changing, however, as Arab donors develop a domestic industrial base. For example, the Saudi Fund has recently changed its Charter in order to allow for the financing and guarantee of non-oil exports alongside the financing of development projects (Saudi Fund 2002). The Arab Bank for Economic Development in Africa (BADEA) issued a Board of Governors decision in 1997, allowing it to 'intervene in financing Arab African trade' (BADEA 2002). The Islamic Development Bank has a Trade Finance & Promotion Department and established the Islamic Corporation for the Insurance of Investment and Export Credits (IDB 2002).

7 Analysis and discussion of results

1 Arab donors are not included here since we used different DI variables for them.

2 Again, Arab donors are not included in the Table 7.8 since we employed different DI variables to explain their aid allocation.

References

Abrams, B.A. and Lewis, K.A. (1993) 'Human Rights and the Distribution of U.S. Foreign Aid', *Public Choice*, 77: 815–21.

Acemoglu, D., Johnson, S. and Robinson, J.A. (2001a) 'The Colonial Origins of Comparative Development: An Empirical Investigation', *American Economic Review*, 91: 1369–401.

Acemoglu, D., Johnson, S. and Robinson, J.A. (2001b) *Reversal of Fortune: Geography and Institutions in the Making of the Modern World Income Distribution*, Working Paper, Berkeley: Massachusetts Institute of Technology and University of California.

Achilli, M. and Khaldi, M. (eds) (1984) *The Role of the Arab Development Funds in the World Economy*, London and Sydney: Croom Helm.

AFESD (1999) *Annual Report*, Kuwait: Arab Fund for Economic and Social Development.

Al-Ani, A. (1984) 'OPEC Aid to Developing Countries', in Achilli, M. and Khaldi, M. (eds) *The Role of the Arab Development Funds in the World Economy*, London and Sydney: Croom Helm, pp. 40–5.

Alesina, A. and Dollar, D. (2000) 'Who Gives Foreign Aid to Whom and Why?', *Journal of Economic Growth*, 5: 33–63.

Alesina, A. and Weder, B. (2000) *Do Corrupt Governments Receive Less Foreign Aid?*, Mimeo, Cambridge, MA and Basel: Harvard University and University of Basel.

Al-Humaidi, B. (1984) 'The Kuwait Fund for Arab Economic Development', in Achilli, M. and Khaldi, M. (eds) *The Role of the Arab Development Funds in the World Economy*, London and Sydney: Croom Helm, pp. 46–58.

Allen, T. and Weinhold, D. (2000) 'Dropping the Debt for the New Millennium: Is it Such a Good Idea?', *Journal of International Development*, 12: 857–76.

Amemiya, T. (1985) *Advanced Econometrics*, Cambridge, MA: Harvard University Press.

Anyadike-Danes, M.K. and Anyadike-Danes, M.N. (1992) 'The Geographic Allocation of the European Development Fund Under the Lomé Conventions', *World Development*, 29: 1647–61.

Apodaca, C. and Stohl, M. (1999) 'United States Human Rights Policy and Foreign Assistance', *International Studies Quarterly*, 43: 185–98.

Arase, D. (1995) *Buying Power – The Political Economy of Japan's Foreign Aid*, London: Boulder.

Arvin, B.M. and Drews, T. (2001) 'Are There Biases in German Bilateral Aid Allocations?', *Applied Economics Letters*, 8: 173–7.

BADEA (2002) *Website*, www.badea.org, Khartoum: Arab Bank for Economic Development in Africa.

Berg, E. (1997) 'Dilemmas in Donor Aid Strategies', in Gwin, C. and Nelson, J.M. (eds) *Perspectives on Aid and Development*, Baltimore: Johns Hopkins University Press, pp. 79–94.

Bowles, P. (1987) 'The Political Economy of UK Foreign Aid', *International-Review-of-Applied-Economics*, 1: 225–40.

Bowles, P. (1989) 'Recipient Needs and Donor Interests in the Allocation of EEC Aid to Developing Countries', *Canadian Journal of Development Studies*, 10: 7–19.

Bräutigam, D. (2000) *Aid Dependence and Governance*, Washington, DC: American University.

Breen, R. (1996) *Regression Models: Censored, Sample-Selected, or Truncated Data*, London: SAGE.

Burnside, C. and Dollar, D. (1997) *Aid, Policies and Growth*, Policy Research Working Paper 1777, Washington, DC: World Bank.

Burnside, C. and Dollar, D. (2000) 'Aid, Policies, and Growth', *American Economic Review*, 90: 847–68.

Carleton, D. and Stohl, M. (1987) 'The Role of Human Rights in U.S. Foreign Assistance Policy: A Critique and Reappraisal', *American Journal of Political Science*, 31: 1002–18.

Cassen, R. (1994) *Does Aid Work?* (1st edn, 1986), Oxford: Clarendon Press.

Chang, C.C., Fernandez-Arias, E. and Serven, L. (1998) *Measuring Aid Flows: A New Approach*, Mimeo, Washington, DC: World Bank.

CIA (2001) *World Fact Book*, Washington, DC: Central Intelligence Agency.

Cingranelli, D.L. and Pasquarello, T.E. (1985) 'Human Rights Practices and the Distribution of U.S. Foreign Aid to Latin American Countries', *American Journal of Political Science*, 29: 539–63.

Cingranelli, D.L. and Richards, D.L. (1999) 'Measuring the Level, Pattern and Sequence of Government Respect for Physical Integrity Rights', *International Studies Quarterly*, 43: 407–17.

Clark, D.P. (1992) 'Distributions of Official Development Assistance Among Developing Country Aid Recipients', *Developing Economies*, 33: 189–97.

Collier, P. (1997) 'The Failure of Conditionality', in Gwin, C. and Nelson, J.M. (eds) *Perspectives on Aid and Development*, Baltimore: Johns Hopkins University Press, pp. 51–77.

Collier, P. and Dollar, D. (1999) *Aid Allocation and Poverty Reduction*, Policy Research Working Paper 2041, Washington, DC: World Bank.

Collier, P. and Dollar, D. (2001) 'Can the World Cut Poverty in Half? How Policy Reform and Effective Aid can Meet International Development Goals', *World Development*, 29: 1787–802.

Cragg, J.G. (1971) 'Some Statistical Models for Limited Dependent Variables with Application to the Demand for Durable Goods', *Econometrica*, 39: 829–44.

Crawford, G. (2000) *Foreign Aid and Political Reform – A Comparative Analysis of Democracy Assistance and Political Conditionality*, Basingstoke: Palgrave.

Davenport, M. (1971) 'The Allocation of Foreign Aid: A Cross Section Study, with Special Reference to the Pearson Commission Report', *Bulletin of Economic Research*, 22: 26–41.

Dijkstra, A.G. (2002) 'The Effectiveness of Policy Conditionality: Eight Country Experiences', *Development and Change*, 33: 307–34.

Dowling, J.M. and Hiemenz, U. (1985) 'Biases in the Allocation of Foreign Aid: Some New Evidence', *World Development*, 13: 535–41.

Dudley, L. and Montmarquette, C. (1976) 'A Model of the Supply of Bilateral Foreign Aid', *American Economic Review*, 66: 132–42.

Dutch Ministry of Foreign Affairs (2001) *Africa Policy*, Den Haag: Dutch Ministry of Foreign Affairs.

Easterly, W. (1999) 'Life During Growth', *Journal of Economic Growth*, 4: 239–76.

Easterly, W. (2001) *Inequality Does Cause Underdevelopment*, Mimeo, Washington, DC: World Bank.

Encyclopedia Britannica (2001) *Britannica Book of the Year*, Chicago: Encyclopedia Britannica.

Engerman, S.L., Haber, S.H. and Sokoloff, K.L. (2001) *Inequality, Institutions, and Differential Paths of Growth Among New World Economies*, Working Paper, University of Rochester, Stanford University, University of California, Los Angeles and National Bureau of Economic Research.

Ensign, M.M. (1992) *Doing Good or Doing Well? Japan's Foreign Aid Program*, New York: Columbia University Press.

EU Council of Ministers (1991) *Resolution of the Council and of the Member States Meeting in the Council on Human Rights, Democracy and Development*, 28 November 1991, Doc. no. 10107/91, Brussels: European Commission.

European Community (2001) *The European Community External Cooperation Programmes. Policies, Management and Distribution*, Brussels: European Community.

Freedom House (2000) *Freedom in the World*, New York: Freedom House.

Frey, B.S. and Schneider, F. (1986) 'Competing Models of International Lending Activity', *Journal of Development Economics*, 20: 225–45.

Gallup, J.I. and Sachs, J. (1999) *Geography and Economic Development*, Mimeo, Cambridge, MA: Harvard University.

Gallup, John L., Jeffrey D. Sachs and Andrew D. Mellinger (1999) 'Geography and Economic Development', *International Regional Science Review*, 22: 179–232.

Gang, I.N. and Lehman, J.A. (1990) 'New Directions or Not: USAID in Latin America', *World Development*, 18: 723–32.

Gartzke, E., Jo, D.J. and Tucker, R. (1999) *The Similarity of UN Policy Positions, 1946–96*, www.vanderbilt.edu/~rtucker/data/affinity/un/similar.

Geiger, R. and Pohl, W. (1954) 'Eine Neue Wandkarte der Klimagebiete der Erde nach W. Köppens Klassifikation', *Erdkunde*, 8: 58–61.

Gibney, M. (2002) *Political Terror Scales Dataset*, Asheville: University of North Carolina.

Gillies, D. (1999) *Between Principle and Practice. Human Rights in North-South Relations*, Montreal: McGill-Queen's University Press.

Gleditsch, K. (2001) *Expanded Trade and GDP Data*, San Diego: University of California.

Gounder, R. (1994) 'Empirical Results of Aid Motivations: Australia's Bilateral Aid Program', *World Development*, 22: 99–113.

Gounder, R. (1995) 'Non-Nested Models of Australia's Overseas Aid Program', *Applied Economics*, 27: 609–21.

Gounder, R. and Doessel, D.P. (1994) 'Population and Middle-Income Biases in Australia's Bilateral Aid: Some Empirical Results', *Development Policy Review*, 12: 29–44.

Grilli, E. and Riess, M. (1992) 'EC Aid to Associated Countries: Distribution and Determinants', *Weltwirtschaftliches Archiv*, 128: 202–20.

Gulhati, R. and Nallari, R. (1988) 'Reform of Foreign Aid Policies: The Issue of Inter-Country Allocation in Africa', *World Development*, 16: 1167–84.

Gurr, T.R. and Jaggers, K. (2000) *Polity98 Project*, University of Maryland (online available at www.bsos.umd.edu/cidcm/polity).

Hansen, H. and Tarp, F. (2000) 'Aid and Growth Regressions', *Journal of Development Economics*, 64: 547–70.

Hansen, H. and Tarp, F. (2001) 'Aid Effectiveness Disputed', *Journal of International Development*, 12: 375–98.

Hansen, H. and White, H. (2000a) 'Aid Allocation, Poverty Reduction and the Assessing Aid Report', *Journal of International Development*, 12: 399–412.

Hansen, H. and White, H. (2000b) 'Assessing Aid: A Manifesto for Aid in the 21st Century', *Oxford Development Studies*, 28: 5–17.

Heckman, J. (1979) 'Sample Selection Bias as a Specification Error', *Econometrica*, 47: 153–61.

Henderson, E.A. and Tucker, R. (2001) 'Clear and Present Strangers: The Clash of Civilizations and International Conflict', *International Studies Quarterly*, 45: 317–38.

Hermes, N. and Lensink, R. (2001) 'Changing the Conditions for Development Aid: A New Paradigm?', *Journal of Development Studies*, 37: 1–16.

Hicks, N. and Streeten, P. (1979) 'Indicators of Development: The Search for a Basic Needs Yardstick', *World Development*, 7: 567–80.

Hopkins, R.F. (2000) 'Political Economy of Foreign Aid', in Tarp, F. (ed.) *Foreign Aid and Development: Lessons Learnt and Directions for the Future*, London: Routledge, pp. 423–49.

Hout, W. (2002) 'Good Governance and Aid: Selectivity Criteria in Development Assistance', *Development and Change*, 33: 511–27.

Humaidan, S.H. (1984) 'The Activities of the Saudi Fund for Development', in Achilli, M. and Khaldi, M. (eds) *The Role of the Arab Development Funds in the World Economy*, London and Sydney: Croom Helm, pp. 59–66.

Hunter, S. (1984) *OPEC and the Third World*, London and Sydney: Croom Helm.

ICRG (2002) *The Rating System*, http://icrgonline.com.

IDA (1997) *IDA in Action 1993–1996*, Washington, DC: World Bank.

IDA (2002a) *How IDA Resources are Allocated*, www.worldbank.org/ida/idalloc.htm (accessed on 12 March 2002).

IDA (2002b) *Country Assessments and IDA Allocations*, Washington, DC: World Bank.

IDB (2002) *Website*, www.isdb.org, Jeddah: Islamic Development Bank.

Imady, M. (1984) 'Patterns of Arab Economic Aid to Third World Countries', *Arab Studies Quarterly*, 6: 70–123.

IMF (2000) *World Financial Statistics on CD-Rom*, Washington, DC: International Monetary Fund.

Isenman, P. (1976) 'Biases in Aid Allocations Against Poorer and Larger Countries', *World Development*, 44:631–41.

Israel Ministry of Foreign Affairs (2000) *Israel's Diplomatic Missions Abroad*, Jerusalem: Ministry of Foreign Affairs.

Japan MOFA (1992) *Japan's Official Development Assistance Charter*, Tokyo: Ministry of Foreign Affairs.

Kanbur, R. (2000) 'Aid, Conditionality and Debt in Africa', in Tarp, F. (ed.) *Foreign Aid and Development: Lessons Learnt and Directions for the Future*, London: Routledge, pp. 409–22.

Karatnycky, A. (1999) *Freedom in the World. The Annual Survey of Political Rights & Civil Liberties 1998–1999*, New York: Freedom House.

Karunaratne, N.D. (1980) 'An Analysis of Contemporary Australian Aid Strategy', *Economic Activity*, 23: 15–21.

Katada, S.N. (1997) 'Two Aid Hegemons: Japanese–US Interaction and Aid Allocation to Latin America and the Caribbean', *World Development*, 25: 931–45.

Kaufmann, D., Kraay, A. and Zoido-Lobatón, P. (1999a) *Aggregating Governance Indicators*, Policy Research Working Paper 2195, Washington, DC: World Bank.

Kaufmann, D., Kraay, A. and Zoido-Lobatón, P. (1999b) *Governance Matters*, Mimeo, Washington, DC: World Bank.

Keenleyside, T.A. and Serkasevich, N. (1989) 'Canada's Aid and Human Rights Observance: Measuring the Relationship', *International Journal*, 14: 138–69.

Kennedy, P. (1992) *A Guide to Econometrics*, 3rd edn, Oxford: Blackwell.

Khader, B. (1984) 'The Afro-Arab Alliance: An Economic Strategy for the 1980s', in Achilli, M. and Khaldi, M. (eds) *The Role of the Arab Development Funds in the World Economy*, London and Sydney: Croom Helm, pp. 155–93.

Khaldi, M. (1984) 'Arab Aid in the World Economy', in Achilli, M. and Khaldi, M. (eds) *The Role of the Arab Development Funds in the World Economy*, London and Sydney: Croom Helm, pp. 7–39.

Killick, R. (1998) *Aid and the Political Economy of Policy Change*, London and New York: Routledge.

King, G. (1986) 'How Not to Lie with Statistics: Avoiding Common Mistakes in Quantitative Political Science', *American Journal of Political Science*, 30: 666–87.

King, G. and Zeng, L. (2001) 'Improving Forecasts of State Failure', *World Politics*, 53: 623–58.

La Porta, Rafael, Florencio Lopez-de-Silanes, Andrei Shleifer and Robert Vishny (1999) 'The Quality of Government', *Journal of Law, Economics & Organization* 15: 222–79.

Lancaster, C. (2000) *Aid to Africa – So Much to Do, So Little Done*, Chicago: University of Chicago Press.

Larson, D.A. and Wilford, W.T. (1979) 'The Physical Quality of Life Index: A Useful Indicator?', *World Development*, 7: 581–4.

Leandro, J.E., Schafer, H. and Frontini, G. (1999) 'Towards a More Effective Conditionality: An Operational Framework', *World Development*, 27: 285–99.

Lensink, R. and White, H. (2001) 'Are There Negative Returns to Aid?', *Journal of Development Studies*, 37: 42–65.

Leung, S.F. and Yu, S. (1996) 'On the Choice Between Sample Selection and Two-Part Models', *Journal of Econometrics*, 72: 197–229.

Llavador, H.G. and Roemer, J.E. (2001) 'An Equal-Opportunity Approach to the Allocation of International Aid', *Journal of Development Economics*, 64: 147–71.

Lloyd, R., McGillivray, M. and Osei, R. (2001) *Problems with Pooling in Panel Data Analysis for Developing Countries: The Case of Aid and Trade Relationships*, CREDIT Research Paper 01/14, University of Nottingham: Centre for Research in Economic Development and International Trade.

Lloyd, R., McGillivray, M., Morrissey, O. and Osei, R. (2000) 'Does Aid Create Trade? An Investigation for European Donors and African Recipients', *European Journal of Development Research*, 12: 107–23.

Lumsdaine, D.H. (1993) *Moral Vision in International Politics – The Foreign Aid Regime, 1949–1989*, Princeton, New Jersey: Princeton University Press.

McArthur, J.W. and Sachs, J.D. (2001) *Institutions and Geography: Comment on Acemoglu, Johnson and Robinson (2000)*, Working Paper 8114, Washington, DC: National Bureau of Economic Research.

McCann, J.A. and Gibney, M. (1996) 'An Overview of Political Terror in the Developing World, 1980–1991', in Stuart S. Nagel (ed.) *Human Rights and Developing Countries*, Greenwich and London: JAI Press, pp. 15–27.

McGillivray, M. (1989) 'The Allocation of Aid Among Developing Countries: A Multi-Donor Analysis Using a Per Capita Aid Index', *World Development*, 17: 561–8.

McGillivray, M. and Oczkowski, E. (1991) 'Modelling the Allocation of Australian Bilateral Aid: A Two-Part Sample Selection Approach', *Economic Record*, 67: 147–52.

McGillivray, M. and Oczkowski, E. (1992) 'A Two-Part Sample Selection Model of British Bilateral Aid Allocation', *Applied Economics*, 24: 1311–19.

McKinlay, R.D. and Little, R. (1977) 'A Foreign Policy Model of U.S. Bilateral Aid Allocation', *World Politics*, 30: 58–86.

McKinlay, R.D. and Little, R. (1978a) 'The French Aid Relationship: A Foreign Policy Model of the Distribution of French Bilateral Aid, 1964–70', *Development and Change*, 9: 459–78.

McKinlay, R.D. and Little, R. (1978b) 'The German Aid Relationship: A Test of the Recipient Need and the Donor Interest Models of the Distribution of German Bilateral Aid 1961–70', *European Journal of Political Research*, 6: 235–57.

McKinlay, R.D. and Little, R. (1978c) 'A Foreign-Policy Model of the Distribution of British Bilateral Aid, 1960–70', *British Journal of Political Science*, 8: 313–32.

McKinlay, R.D. and Little, R. (1979) 'The US Aid Relationship: A Test of the Recipient Need and the Donor Interest Model', *Political Studies*, 27: 236–50.

Maddala, G.S. (1985) 'A Survey of the Literature on Selectivity Bias as it Pertains to Health Care Markets', *Advances in Health Economics and Health Services Research*, 6: 3–18.

Maddala, G.S. (1992) 'Censored Data Models', in Eatwell, J., Milgate, M. and Newman, P. (eds) *The New Palgrave Econometrics*, London: Macmillan, pp. 54–7.

Maddala, G.S. (2000) *An Introduction to Econometrics*, London: Macmillan.

Maizels, A. and Nissanke, M.K. (1984) 'Motivations for Aid to Developing Countries', *World Development*, 12: 879–900.

Manning, W.G., Duan, N. and Rogers, W.H. (1987) 'Monte Carlo Evidence on the Choice Between Sample Selection and Two-Part Models', *Journal of Econometrics*, 35: 59–82.

Masters, W.A. and Mcmillan, M.S. (2001) 'Climate and Scale in Economic Growth', *Journal of Economic Growth*, 6: 167–86.

Meenai, S.A. (1989) *The Islamic Development Bank – A Case Study of Islamic Co-operation*, London and New York: Kegan Paul.

Mertz, Robert Anton and Pamela MacDonald Mertz (1983) *Arab Aid to Sub-Saharan Africa*, Boulder: Westview.

Ministry of Foreign Affairs (2000) *Israel's Diplomatic Missions Abroad*, Jerusalem: Ministry of Foreign Affairs.

Moon, B.E. (1991) *The Political Economy of Basic Human Needs*, Ithaca: Cornell University Press.

Moon, B.E. and Dixon, W.J. (1992) 'Basic Needs and Growth-Welfare Trade-Offs', *International Studies Quarterly*, 36: 191–212.

Morawetz, D. (1979) *Twenty-five Years of Economic Development 1950 to 1975*, Baltimore: Johns Hopkins University Press.

Morris, D.M. (1979) *Measuring the Condition of the World's Poor – The Physical Quality of Life Index*, published for the Overseas Development Council, New York: Pergamon Press.

Morris, M.D. (1996) *Measuring the Changing Condition of the World's Poor: The Physical Quality of Life Index, 1960–1990*, Working Paper 23/24, Providence: Brown University.

Mosley, P. (1980) 'Models of the Aid Allocation Process: A Comment on McKinlay and Little', *Political Studies*, 29: 245–53.

Neumayer, E. (1999) *Weak Versus Strong Sustainability: Exploring the Limits of Two Opposing Paradigms*, Cheltenham: Edward Elgar.

Neumayer, E. (2000) 'Resource Accounting in Measures of Unsustainability: Challenging the World Bank's Conclusions', *Environmental and Resource Economics*, 15: 257–78.

Neumayer, E. (2003a) 'The Determinants of Aid Allocation by Regional Development Banks and United Nations Agencies', *International Studies Quarterly*, 47.

Neumayer, E. (2003b) 'Is Respect for Human Rights Rewarded? An Analysis of Total Bilateral and Multilateral Aid Flows', *Human Rights Quarterly*, 25.

Neumayer, E. (2003c) 'Do Human Rights Matter in Bilateral Aid Allocation? A Quantitative Analysis of 21 Donor Countries', *Social Science Quarterly*, 84.

Neumayer, E. (2003d) 'What Factors Determine the Allocation of Aid by Arab Countries and Multilateral Agencies?', *Journal of Development Studies*, 39: 133–46.

Neumayer, E. (2003e) *Arab-related Bilateral and Multilateral Sources of Development Finance: Issues, Trends, and the Way Forward*, Discussion Paper No. 2002/96, Helsinki: United Nations University, World Institute for Development Economics Research. Also published in WORLD ECONOMY (forthcoming).

Noël, A. and Thérien, J.-P. (1995) 'From Domestic to International Justice: The Welfare State and Foreign Aid', *International Organization*, 49: 523–53.

Nonneman, G. (1988), *Development, Administration and Aid in the Middle East*, London and New York: Routledge.

OECD (1994) *DAC Orientations on Participatory Development and Good Governance*, Paris: Organisation for Economic Co-operation and Development.

OECD (2001) *DAC Guidelines Poverty Reduction*, Paris: Organisation of Economic Co-operation and Development.

OECD (2002a) *Statistical Compendium on CD-Rom*, Paris: Organisation for Economic Co-operation and Development.

OECD (2002b) *Development Co-operation – 2001 Report*, Paris: Organisation for Economic Co-operation and Development.

OECD (2002c) *Source OECD* data, Paris: Organisation for Economic Co-operation and Economic Development.

OFID (2002) *Website*, www.opecfund.org, Vienna: OPEC Fund for International Development.

Parker, P.M. (1997) *National Cultures of the World – A Statistical Reference*, Westport: Greenwood Press.

Payaslian, S. (1996) *U.S. Foreign Economic and Military Aid – The Reagan and Bush Administrations*, Lanham: University Press of America.

Perry, Michael J. (1997) 'Are Human Rights Universal? The Relativist Challenge and Related Matters', *Human Rights Quarterly*, 19: 461–509.

Poe, S.C. (1992) 'Human Rights and Economic Aid Allocation under Ronald Reagan and Jimmy Carter', *American Journal of Political Science*, 36: 147–67.

Poe, S.C. and Sirirangsi, R. (1994) 'Human Rights and U.S. Economic Aid During the Reagan Years', *Social Science Quarterly*, 75: 494–509.

Poe, S.C., Pilatovsky, S., Miller, B. and Ogundele, A. (1994) 'Human Rights and US Foreign Aid Revisited: The Latin American Region', *Human Rights Quarterly*, 16: 539–58.

Porter, R.S. (1986) 'Arab Economic Aid', *Development Policy Review*, 4: 44–68.

Pronk, J.P. (2001) 'Aid as a Catalyst', *Development and Change*, 32: 611–29.

Puhani, P. (2000) 'The Heckman Correction for Sample Selection and its Critique', *Journal of Economic Surveys*, 14: 53–68.

Raffer, K. and Singer, H.W. (1996) *The Foreign Aid Business – Economic Assistance and Development Co-operation*, Cheltenham: Edward Elgar.

Rao, J.M. (1997) 'Ranking Foreign Donors: An Index Combining the Scale and Equity of Aid Giving', *World Development*, 25: 947–61.

San Suu Kyi, A. (1995) 'Transcending the Clash of Cultures: Freedom, Development and Human Worth', *Journal of Democracy*, 6: 11–19.

Saudi Fund (2002) *Website*, www.sfd.gov.sa, Jeddah: Saudi Fund for Development.

Schraeder, P.J., Hook, S.W. and Taylor, B. (1998) 'Clarifying the Foreign Aid Puzzle. A Comparison of American, Japanese, French and Swedish Aid Flows', *World Politics*, 50: 294–323.

Selbervik, H. (1997) *Aid as a Tool for Promotion of Human Rights and Democracy: What can Norway Do?*, Oslo: Norwegian Ministry of Foreign Affairs.

Sen, A.K. (1985) *Commodities and Capabilities*, Amsterdam: North-Holland.

Shihata, Ibrahim F.I. (1982) *The Other Face of OPEC – Financial Assistance to the Third World*, London and New York: Longman.

Signorino, C.S. and Ritter, J.M. (1999) 'Tau-b or Not Tau-b: Measuring the Similarity of Foreign Policy Positions', *International Studies Quarterly*, 43: 115–44.

Simmons, A. (1981) *Arab Foreign Aid*, London and Toronto: Associated University Press.

Singh, A. (2002) 'Aid, Conditionality and Development', *Development and Change*, 33: 295–305.

Sokoloff, K.L. and Engerman, S.L. (2000) 'Institutions, Factor Endowments, and Paths of Development in the New World', *Journal of Economic Perspectives*, 14: 217–32.

Stata (2001) *Stata 7.0 Reference Manual*, College Station: Stata Corporation.

Stokke, O. (ed.) (1989) *Western Middle Powers and Global Poverty – The Determinants of the Aid Policies of Canada, Denmark, the Netherlands, Norway and Sweden*, Uppsala: The Scandinavian Institute of African Studies.

Svensson, J. (1999) 'Aid, Growth and Democracy', *Economics and Politics*, 11: 275–97.

Svensson, J. (2000) 'Foreign Aid and Rent-seeking', *Journal of International Economics*, 51: 437–61.

Svensson, J. (2003) 'Why Conditional Aid Does Not Work and What Can be Done About It?', *Journal of Development Economics*, 70.

Theobald, R. (1997) 'Can Debt be Used to Combat Political Corruption in Africa?', *Crime, Law and Social Change*, 27: 299–314.

Tobin, J. (1958) 'Esimation of Relationships for Limited Dependent Variables', *Econometrica*, 26: 24–36.

Tomaševski, K. (1993) *Development Aid and Human Rights Revisited*, London: Pinter.

Tomaševski, K. (1997) *Between Sanctions and Elections: Aid Donors and Their Human Rights Performance*, London: Pinter.

Trumbull, W.N. and Wall, H.J. (1994) 'Estimating Aid-allocation Criteria with Panel Data', *Economic Journal*, 104: 876–82.

Tsoutsoplides, C. (1991) 'The Determinants of the Geographical Allocation of EC Aid to the Developing Countries', *Applied Economics*, 23: 647–58.

UNDP (1990) *Human Development Report 1990*, New York: United Nations Development Programme.

US Bureau of Arms Control (1995, 1998) *World Military Expenditures and Arms Transfers*, Washington, DC: US Arms Control and Disarmament Agency.

USAID (2002) *U.S. Oversees Loans and Grants Online (Greenbook)*, http://qesdb.cdie.org.

Van den Boogaerde, P. (1991) *Financial Assistance from Arab Countries and Arab Regional Institutions*, Washington, DC: International Monetary Fund.

Vella, F. (1998) 'Estimating Models with Sample Selection Bias: A Survey', *Journal of Human Resources*, 33: 127–69.

Verbeek, M. (2000) *A Guide to Modern Econometrics*, Chichester: John Wiley & Sons.

Wall, H.J. (1995) 'The Allocation of Official Development Assistance', *Journal of Policy Modelling*, 17: 307–14.

Weck-Hannemann, H. (1987) 'Politisch-ökonomische Bestimmungsgründe der Vergabe von Entwicklungshilfe: Eine empirische Untersuchung für die Schweiz', *Schweizerische Zeitschrift für Volkswirtschaft und Statistik*, 123: 501–27.

White, H. and McGillivray, M. (1995) 'How Well is Aid Allocated? Descriptive Measures of Aid Allocation: A Survey of Methodology and Results', *Development and Change*, 26: 163–83.

WHO (2000) *Estimates of Income Per Capita for the World Health Report 2000*, Geneva: World Health Organization.

Woods, N. (2000) 'The Challenge of Good Governance for the IMF and the World Bank Themselves', *World Development*, 28: 823–41.

Wooldridge, J.M. (2002) *Econometric Analysis of Cross Section and Panel Data*, Cambridge, MA: MIT Press.

World Bank (1998) *Assessing Aid: What Works, What Doesn't, and Why*, New York: Oxford University Press.

World Bank (2000) *Country Fixed Factors Database*, Washington, DC: World Bank.

World Bank (2001) *World Development Indicators on CD-Rom*, Washington, DC: World Bank.

Index

Printed in the United States
by Baker & Taylor Publisher Services